The Unlikely Hero of Sobrance
(Sobrance, Slovakia)

By William Leibner and Larry Price

Edited by Ingrid Rockberger

Published by JewishGen

An Affiliate of the Museum of Jewish Heritage - A Living Memorial to the Holocaust
New York

The Unlikely Hero of Sobrance

Authors: William Leibner (Israel) and Larry Price (Israel)
Editor: Ingrid Rockberger (Israel)
Layout: Joel Alpert (Massachusetts, USA)
Cover Design: Nili Goldman (Israel)

Published by JewishGen, Inc.
An Affiliate of the Museum of Jewish Heritage
A Living Memorial to the Holocaust
36 Battery Place, New York, NY 10280

Printed in the United States of America by Lightning Source, Inc.

Library of Congress Control Number (LCCN): 2016952721
ISBN: 978-1-939561-45-9 (hard cover: 210 pages, alk. paper)

Cover photographs: Courtesy of Yad VaShem

JewishGen and the Yizkor-Books-in-Print Project

This book has been published by the **Yizkor-Books-in-Print Project,** as part of the **Yizkor Book Project** of **JewishGen, Inc**.

JewishGen, Inc. is a non-profit organization founded in 1987 as a resource for Jewish genealogy. Its website [www.jewishgen.org] serves as an international clearinghouse and resource center to assist individuals who are researching the history of their Jewish families and the places where they lived. JewishGen provides databases, facilitates discussion groups, and coordinates projects relating to Jewish genealogy and the history of the Jewish people. In 2003, JewishGen became an affiliate of the **Museum of Jewish Heritage - A Living Memorial to the Holocaust** in New York.

The **JewishGen Yizkor Book Project** was organized to make more widely known the existence of Yizkor (Memorial) Books written by survivors and former residents of various Jewish communities throughout the world. Later, volunteers connected to the different destroyed communities began cooperating to have these books translated from the original language— usually Hebrew or Yiddish—into English, thus enabling a wider audience to have access to the valuable information contained within them. As each chapter of these books was translated, it was posted on the JewishGen website and made available to the general public.

The **Yizkor-Books-in-Print Project** began in 2011 as an initiative to print and publish Yizkor Books that had been fully translated, so that hard copies would be available for purchase by the descendants of these communities and also by scholars, universities, synagogues, libraries, and museums.

These Yizkor books have been produced almost entirely through the volunteer effort of researchers from around the world, assisted by donations from private individuals. The books are printed and sold at near cost, so as to make them as affordable as possible. Our goal is to make this important genre of Jewish literature and history available in English in book form, so that people can have the personal histories of their ancestral towns on their bookshelves for themselves and for their children and grandchildren.

A list of all published translated Yizkor Books in the project with prices and ordering information can be found at:

http://www.jewishgen.org/Yizkor/ybip.html

Lance Ackerfeld, Yizkor Book Project Manager

Joel Alpert, Yizkor-Book-in-Print Project Coordinator

JewishGen
Yizkor Book Project

This book is presented by the
Yizkor Books in Print Project
Project Coordinator: Joel Alpert

Part of the
Yizkor Books Project of JewishGen, Inc.
Project Manager: Lance Ackerfeld

These books have been produced solely through volunteer effort
of individuals from around the world. The books are printed and
sold at near cost, so as to make them as affordable as possible.

Our goal is to make this history and important genre of Jewish
literature available in English in book form so that people can have
the near-personal histories of their ancestral towns on their bookshelves for themselves and for their children and grandchildren.

Any donations to the Yizkor Books Project are appreciated.

Please send donations to:
Yizkor Book Project
JewishGen
36 Battery Place
New York, NY 10280

JewishGen, Inc. is an affiliate of the
Museum of Jewish Heritage
A Living Memorial to the Holocaust

Preface

Following World War II, the surviving Jews of Eastern Europe, especially Poland, felt insecure and threatened. The Shoah survivors that returned from the labor and concentration camps and those that returned from Russia began to disappear without a trace. No papers, no visas, no passports and yet thousands moved mainly to Czechoslovakia and onwards to Germany and Austria. I was amongst those Polish Jews who left Poland without leaving a trace.

I was always wondering who organized, financed, and transported us from Poland to Central Europe. There was no Jewish government or Agency that officially assumed this task.

Another question: why did Czechoslovakia consent to this massive transfer of people? True, the Czech government was friendly and well-disposed to Jews but it required a large outlay of money and a strong will to resist British demands to close all Czech borders to Jews. Czechoslovakia stood its ground.

We wanted to know who specifically stood behind these decisions and enabled about 250,000 Jews to reach the German and Austrian D.P. camps in the American-occupied zones. Zdenek Toman was one of the important executors of this plan from his position in the Czech Ministry of Interior. He saved thousands of Jews from further anti-Semitic hardships and pogroms.

Little is known about this corner of history; therefore, we decided to devote a book to him and memorialize his endeavors for which he paid a heavy price.

William Leibner and Larry Price, Jerusalem, Israel

Acknowledgements

Avner Shalev, Chairman of the Yad Vashem Directorate, Rachel Barkai, Director of Commemoration and Public Relations, Yad Vashem; Dr. Robert Rozette, Director of Yad Vashem library; Rachel Cohen, Secretary of Yad Vashem library; Mimi Ash at the Yad Vashem Media Center in Jerusalem; David Sinai, Head of Human Resources Department, and all of Yad Vashem staff at the various research stations in Jerusalem and Dr. Daniel Uziel of the archive division at Yad Vashem, the library staff at Yad Vashem.

Many thanks are in order to my wife, Claudette Leibner, who helped with the artistic layout of the cover page.

Thanks to Linda Price for helping to put the material in the proper perspective.

Special thanks are in order for Emil Leibner who constantly provided technical media assistance. We also want to express our thanks to all the translators of the various documents that enabled us to write the book.

Special mention is in order for Dr. Zvi Fine who provided background material and guidance in the area of Joint operations in Europe.

Ingrid Rockberger deserves a special citation for the hard work of shaping the *Unlikely Hero of Sobrance* into a presentable and readable story.

We would also like to thank all the people that were interviewed and extended cooperation and goodwill to the project.

William Leibner and Larry Price (Jerusalem)

Geopolitical Information:

Sobrance, Slovakia: <u>48°45' N, 22°11' E</u>

Located in Eastern Slovakia, 43 miles E of Košice (Kassa), 11 miles NNW of Uzhhorod (Ungvár).

Alternate names for the town are: Sobrance [Slovakian], Szobráncz [Hungarian], Szobránc [Hungarian], Sobranz [German]

Jewish Population in 1900: 349 (in 1880), 395 (in 1941)

Period	Town	District	Province	Country
Before WWI (c. 1900):	Szobráncz	Ung	Slovakia	Hungary
Between the wars (c. 1930):	Sobrance		Slovakia	Czechoslovakia
After WWII (c. 1950):	Sobrance			Czechoslovakia
Today (c. 2000):	Sobrance			Slovakia

Notes to the Reader:

A list of this book and all books available in the Yizkor-Book-In-Print Project along with prices is available at:

http://www.jewishgen.org/Yizkor/ybip.html

Table of Contents

Chapter   **Page**

     Introduction   1

  I The Goldberger Family   12

  II Toman's Background   26

  III The Transit Station Czechoslovakia   40

  IV The Human Flood   54

  V The Children's Transport   71

  VI Britain at War with the Jews   100

  VII The Mass Exit Continues   115

  VIII The Goldberger Family Reunites   129

  IX Toman's Downfall   136

  X The Escape   148

  XI The Trial   155

  XII Toman the Jewish Benefactor   164

  XIII Ivan Toman   175

     Appendix: Partial List of Sobrance Jews   181

     Bibliography   188

Notes

The Unlikely Hero of Sobrance

by William Leibner and Larry Price

The picture on the cover represents Zdenek Toman-Goldberger looking from behind a barred window as the trains with Jewish refugees leave Czechoslovakia on their way to Austrian and German D.P. (displaced persons) camps located predominantly in the American military occupied zones.

The large sign on the passenger car reads: 'Repatriacni Vlak' or repatriation train.

The letters CSD stand for 'Ceskolovenske Statni Drany', or Czechoslovak State Railways.

In Memoriam

Pesla/Paula Gutman/Toman

Ivan Toman

and

Zdenek Toman

To All the Members of the

Mossad, Brichah, Jewish Brigade

Haganah, Joint, Jewish Soldiers,

Jewish Volunteers

Who Fell in the Line of Duty While

Helping the Mass Exodus of Jews

From Eastern Europe to the Shores

of the Holy Land

See Zdenek Toman regarding Jewish matters said: Jan Masaryk, Czech Foreign Minister to Gaynor Jacobson. "If Toman is on your side…the frontiers of Czechoslovakia will be open to your Jews"

Tad Szulc, "The Secret Alliance" p.143

"Without Zdenek Toman, there would have never been a massive transfer of East European Jewish survivors" said Florence Jacobson, a social worker for the Joint in Prague and wife of Israel Gaynor, joint director of Prague in a film appearance in the movie entitled "The Bricha" produced by Martin Smok, Czech film maker and historian.

**Asher Zelig Goldberger/
Zoltan Goldberger/
Zoltan Toman /
Zdenek Toman
Zdenek Toman/Goldberger**

Introduction

In June 1948 Zdenek Toman, once one of the most feared and powerful men in post-War Czechoslovakia, was sitting in a Prague jail, accused of running a ring of black market operations for personal gain. Analysts believe the newly installed Communist government run by Klement Gottwald trumped up most of the accusations. Toman was told to expect a death sentence.

In a scattered sequence of events, the arrest warrant for Toman was issued in January of 1948 but before he was officially arrested he was sent on a forced "vacation" to a rest home outside of Prague. Held under non-declared house arrest, Toman was cut off from any contact with his family or friends. His wife, Paula, went to Toman's former nominal boss, the Interior Minister Nosek, for information. None was forthcoming. She was told not to worry. While Toman was recovering from an undiagnosed illness, the Czech Communist Party with the help of the Russian secret service strengthened their grip over Czechoslovakia. When Toman was finally released in May he had only a few days before the arrest warrant was finally executed in June, and Toman was brought to jail.

Czechoslovakia's West-leaning Foreign Minister Jan Masaryk, a Liberal Democrat, was already dead. He died on March 10, 1948. Officially he had committed suicide just after the Communist take-over in February 1948. But the circumstances of his death were murky, including a suicide note of questionable veracity. The only thing that was certain was Masaryk's fall from the window of his apartment to the sidewalk several stories below. To this day, nobody knows what exactly happened to Masaryk.

Tad Szulc, author of the book "Secret Alliance" believes that Toman was part of the Soviet clean-up of any possible resistance to the Communist rule in Czechoslovakia. Toman was much too powerful a figure to be allowed to remain in power. He was too involved with Western agencies notably the UNRRA (United Nations Relief and Rehabilitation Administration) and the JDC (American Joint Distribution Committee). Even though Toman had been an ardent Communist, and trained by the KGB how to set-up the Czech secret police, he was considered a liability. He knew too much about too many people in power. He met the British and American ambassadors who were protesting the open doors of Czechoslovakia that enabled about 250,000 East European Jews to leave their temporary homes and reach the D.P. camps. He knew many of those had benefited by the black-market deals Toman had pulled off while raising money for the Czech Communist party and for some party officials. Some had expensive rugs in their homes provided by Toman, others jewelry for their wives, not to mention the whiskey and cigars as rare as water in the desert for most Czechs.

While in jail, awaiting his trial, Toman was given the shocking news that his beautiful wife Paula, a pharmacist, had committed suicide, leaping from her third-floor apartment's balcony, much as Jan Masaryk was said to have done a few months earlier. Paula jumped holding her hand-bag, with a suicide note inside of it, wearing high-heeled shoes, leaving her 18 month old son Ivan. Observers believe that Paula Toman was killed to show her husband that he better cooperate with the authorities who were preparing a show trial reminiscent of the famous Stalin show trials of "Boukharine" and others. His son Ivan also disappeared, never to be seen again.

Toman's reaction was totally unexpected. He planned and executed his escape from jail and then from Czechoslovakia. He reached Venezuela[1] where his brother lived. He amassed a fortune and became a large financial donor to Israel. He showed up at Israel's Ben Gurion University of the Negev where he dedicated a building for $5 million, receiving an honorary doctorate on the same stage as former U.S. Secretary of State Alexander Haig. For a man who ran the Czech secret police, a clone of the KGB, Toman is a most unlikely hero.

Ministry of Interior of Czechoslovakia in Prague where Zdenek Toman had his office

Polish Jews approach the PolishCzech border

Polish Jews awaiting opening of the border gate at the Czech-Polish border

Czech brichah agents meet in Bratislava, Czechoslovakia in 1946 to coordinate the flow of Jewish transports to Czechoslovakia and from Czechoslovakia.

Jewish children arrive in Prague

Jewish refuges in Czech transit wait for train to take them out of the country.

The train has arrived with the refugees aboard

Chapter I
The Goldberger family

We decided to begin the story by providing short biographical sketches of the family so that the reader could follow the story. The extended Goldberger family has many active participants and in order to follow them we need a family reference page, notably with name changes. We hope that this unorthodox way of presentation will help the reader to follow the story and receive a better understanding of the period.

Goldberger, David owned a grocery store where liquor was sold in Sobrance, Slovakia. He was very religious and the family was related to Hasidic rabbis. David married Rosalia Thoman. They had eight children. David was deported to the Uzhhorod ghetto by the Germans and Hungarians in March of 1944 and then sent to Auschwitz on May 17th 1944. He perished in the Holocaust.

Goldberger, Rosalia nee Thoman, a native of Sobrance married David Goldberger. She was orthodox and wore a wig. They had eight children. She was deported to the Uzhhorod ghetto by the Germans and Hungarians in March of 1944 and then sent to Auschwitz on May 17,1944.She perished in the Holocaust.

Goldberger, Armin, son of David and Rosalia, born in 1903 in Sobrance. Finished elementary school in Sobrance and high school in Uzhhorod. He studied electrical engineering. He graduated and left Czechoslovakia. In the spring of 1940, he reached Venezuela. He worked all his life as an engineer. He started to work in Venezuela for the Public Works Ministry and later became an independent contractor. He married Suze Eylenbur (a native of Breslau, Germany) and they had two children: Tomas born on August 18, 1940 and a daughter who lives in Palo Alto, California. The family lived in Caracas and had an industrial company named Gexim that dealt with industrial machinery in Caracas. Armin died in 1998 in Venezuela. Tomas Goldberger married Cecilia. Tomas Goldberger and his wife live in Miami, USA.

Goldberger, Baruch, (Jeno) son of David and Rosalia. Born in 1908 in Sobrance. He married Ella Grunfeld. His traces were lost during WWII. Apparently he was drafted into the Hungarian labor battalions and disappeared. Baruch Goldberger married Ella Braunfeld, born in 1914 in Sobrance. She was deported to the Uzhhorod ghetto by the Germans and Hungarians in March of 1944 and then sent to Auschwitz May 17, 1944. She perished in the Holocaust.

Goldberger, Esther, daughter of Baruch and Ella Goldberger born in Sobrance in 1941. Deported to Uzhhorod ghetto by the Germans and Hungarians in March of 1944 and then sent to Auschwitz on May 17, 1944. She perished in the Holocaust.

רשות זכרון לשואה ולגבורה. ירושלים

38.895.

ד ף - ע ד

לרשום חללי השואה והגבורה

ירושלים, רחוב בן־יהודה 12

Goldberger	*[handwritten Hebrew]*	בעברית	1. שם המשפחה בשם ארץ המוצא (באותיות לטיניות)
	Ella	בעברית	2. שם פרטי בשם ארץ המוצא (באותיות לטיניות)
	[handwritten Hebrew]		3. שם האב
	[handwritten Hebrew]		4. שם האם
	1914		5. תאריך הלידה
	Sobrance *[handwritten Hebrew]*		6. מקום וארץ הלידה (גם באותיות לטיניות)
	"		7. מקום המגורים הקבוע (גם באותיות לטיניות)
	[handwritten Hebrew]		8. המקצוע
	[handwritten Hebrew]		9. הנתינות לפני הכבוש הנאצי
	Sobranee *[handwritten Hebrew]*		10. מקומות המגורים במלחמה (גם באותיות לטיניות)
	Aušvic 1944. *[handwritten Hebrew]*		11. מקום המות. הזמן והנסיבות (הפרטים גם באותיות לטיניות)
	1		12. מצב משפחתי
	[handwritten Hebrew]		13. שם האשה ושם משפחתה לפני הנישואין
גילה 30	*[handwritten Hebrew]*		שם הבעל

חוק זכרון השואה והגבורה ־

י ד ו ש ם

תשי"ב 1953

קובע בסעיף מס' 8

שמות הילדים עד גיל 18 שנספו (מעל לגיל זה רשמים זה "יד־עד" מיוחד)	הגיל	המקום והזמן שנספו
[handwritten Hebrew]	3	1944 *[handwritten Hebrew]*

ה ע ר ה : את הילדים יש לרשום ב. דף־העד ־ של אחד ההורים אך לא יותר מפעם אחת.

אני *[handwritten Hebrew]*

קרוב/ת מכר/ה *[handwritten Hebrew]* את *[handwritten Hebrew]*

מצהיר/ה כי בזה כי העדות שמסרתי כאן על פרשיה זו היא נכונה ואמתית, לפי מיטב ידיעתי והכרתי.

אני מבקש/ת להעניק לנ״ל אזרחות־זכרון מטעם מדינת ישראל.

מקום ותאריך *[handwritten Hebrew]*
5./10. 55.

אזרחות ־זכרון הוענקה

מספר אב

לידיעת ,האגף המדעי" בירושלים. רחוב בן־יהודה 12

הייתי בזמן המלחמה במחנה (הסגר. עבודה. השמדה. וכו') _____ בניסו _____

במחתרת _____ ביערות _____ וכו' _____

ואני מוכן למסור עדות על כך. _____ כתבתי _____ חתימת העד _____

Testimony page submitted by a brother of Ella Grunfeld in 1955 to Yad Vashem in Jerusalem

Goldberger, Bossi, daughter of David and Rosalia. Born in Sobrance. Married. Deported to Uzhhorod ghetto by Germans and Hungarians in March of 1944 and then sent to Auschwitz on May 17,1944. She perished in the Holocaust.

Asher Zelig Goldberger

Goldberger Asher Zelig, son of David and Rosalia. Born on March 2, 1909 in Sobrance. Finished elementary school in Sobrance and high school in Uzzhorod. Entered the law faculty of the Charles University in Prague in the winter term of 1927/1928 and graduated in 1933 as an attorney. He joined the Communist party at the University. Married Pesla Gutman on January 26th,1935 in Lodz, Poland. Spent war years in England. Member of the Czech Government in Exile in London. Returned to liberated Czechoslovakia and headed state security office and member of the Czech Repatriation Commission. Helped the American Joint and the Bricha organization to transport thousands of Polish, Hungarian, Rumanian, Czech, Slovak, Ukrainian and Baltic Jews across Czechoslovakia to the D.P. refugee camps in Germany, Austria and Italy. There were about 60,000 Jews in these countries at the end of the war. Toman officially stated that he helped 250,000 Jews reach safety. In 1948 their number reached about 300,000. In 1948 he was arrested but fled to West Germany[2], then to London[3] and later to Venezuela where he joined the family plant of "Gexim" established by his brother Armin. On June 23, 1949 he was condemned to death in absentia and loss of all assets. His appeal to the Czech Supreme Court was rejected on April 3 1950. His wife supposedly committed suicide on May 8, 1948. His son disappeared forever. He married again to Maria Marinadi. He made large contributions to various cultural and educational institutions in Israel namely the Ben Gurion University of Beer Sheba. He was known as Zoltan Toman and was the recipient of many awards on behalf of his activities, in Israel and the USA. Toman was officially rehabilitated following 1989. He died December 20, 1997 in Cabo San Lucas a Mexican resort, later buried in Santa Barbara, California. Eventually buried in Venezuela.

Gutman Pesla, daughter of Mendel Gutman, born in Konskie, Poland on December 25th 1912. She studied pharmacology at the Karlovary University in Prague where she met Zoltan Toman. They married on January 26th, 1935, in Lodz, Poland. The couple later escaped to England where they spent the war years. She worked for the Czech Red Cross in England. Both returned to liberated Czechoslovakia. With the arrest of her husband on April 27, 1948, the Czech security police questioned her; she then supposedly committed suicide by jumping through the window. She fell in the courtyard of her building on May 8, 1948. The janitor reported the incident to the police. Her body was cremated by order of the police. A brother of hers, Zvi Gutman survived the war and reached Israel.

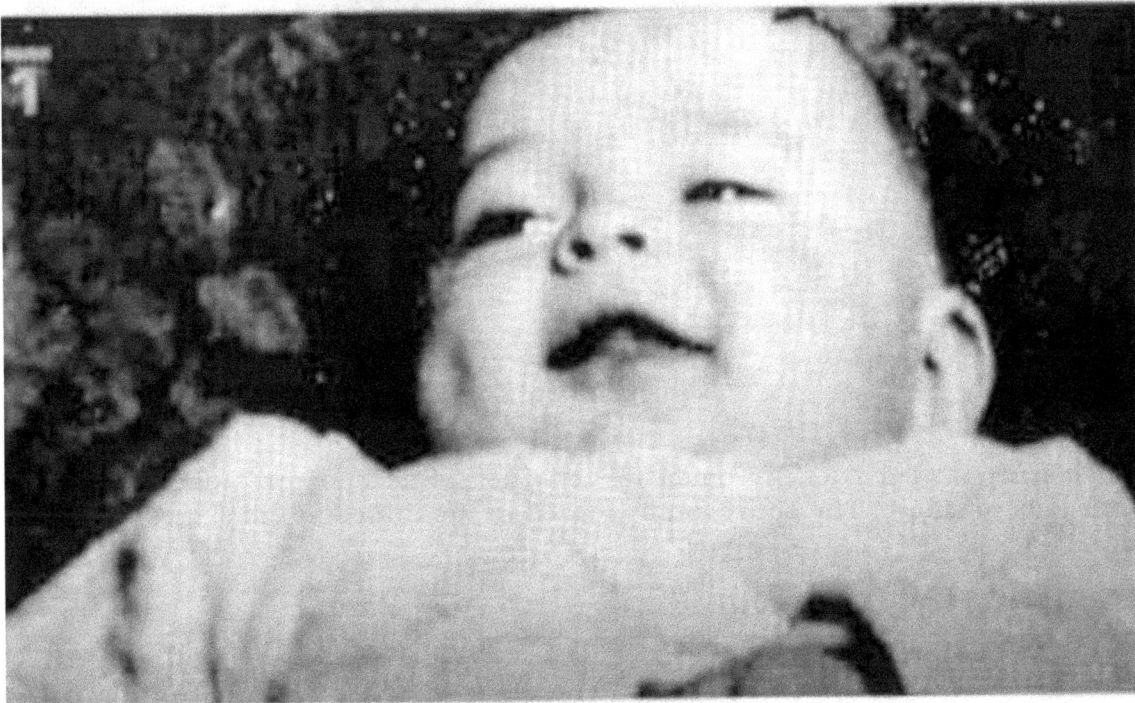

Ivan Toman, the son of Zdenek and Pesla Toman/Goldberger

Ivan Toman was born on October 4, 1947. With his mother's supposed suicide, he was placed in Stvnce a state shelter for infants in Prague. Ivan was constantly moved back and forth until he completely disappeared from sight. The Czech secret police moved him from place to place. The authorities never revealed his whereabouts. All inquiries were ignored or sent to the wrong places. The Czech secret police did on occasion release misleading reports about the boy but no attempt was ever made to return the child to the family or to a normal home for infants.

Maria Marinadi Toman

Maria married Zdenek Toman in Venezuela. She had three daughters by a previous marriage. The entire family moved to the States in the sixties. She died in 2003.

Goldberger, Bella, daughter of David and Rosalia. Born in Sobrance. Married. Deported to Uzhhorod ghetto by Germans and Hungarians in March of 1944 and then sent to Auschwitz on May 17,1944. She perished in the Holocaust.

Goldberger, Klara, daughter of David and Rosalia. Born in Sobrance. Deported to Uzhhorod ghetto by Germans and Hungarians in March of 1944 and then sent to Auschwitz on May 17th 1944. She perished in the Holocaust.

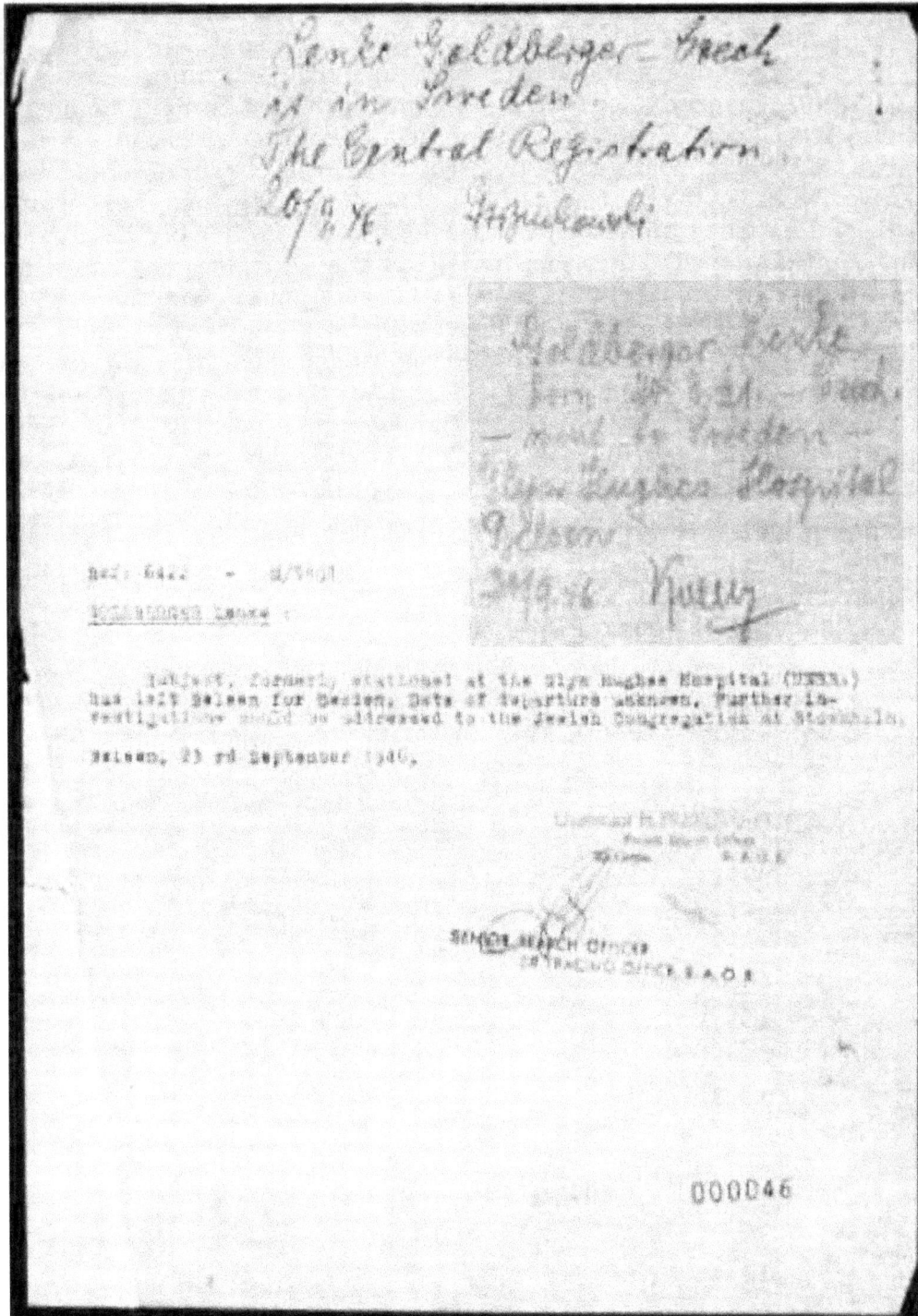

Letter of reply from the International Tracing office in Arolsen, Germany as to the whereabouts of Lenke Goldberger. Notice the remarks written in pencil that state that she was sent to Sweden to recuperate following the war. Information provided by UNRRA

Goldberger, Lenke (Magdalena), daughter of David and Rosalia Goldberger, born on January 20, 1913 in Sobrance. She was sent to Germany to her mother's sister, Fanny Thomann who lived in Germany. She was arrested and sent to the Ravensbruck concentration camp with her aunt in October 1943. She then moved to other camps and wound up in Bergen Belsen concentration camp, where she was liberated by the British. She barely survived and was sent to a Swedish hospital to recuperate. Slowly she regained her health and strength and returned to Prague, Czechoslovakia where her brother Toman was an important official. She also met her sister Aranka in Prague. Lemke took on the last name of Toman and became Lenke Toman. She married Simon Leibovitz, a native of Muncacz, Czechoslovakia. In 1949, they managed to leave Czechoslovakia and reached Caracas Venezuela where her brother Armin Goldberg lived. They lived in Venezuela and were naturalized in Venezuela in 1952. They arrived in New York (Idlewild Airport, now JFK) from Maiquetia, Venezuela, on April 24, 1966, via Pan Am Airways. She passed away on April 21, 1999 and is buried in Santa Barbara, California.

Below is a document sent by the Arolsen Tracing Office to a legal office in Germany regarding the whereabouts of Lenke Goldberger, Red Cross letter from Venezuela indicating Lenke's file as well as all the family members of the Goldberger family in Caracas, Venezuela.

Refugee Identuty Card of Lenke Goldberger , daughter of Dvid and Rosalia Goldberger of Sobrance.

Goldberger, Aranka Goldberger, Aranka / Aurelie, daughter of David and Rosalia, born on April 4th, 1918, in Sobrance. She finished the local school and took some commercial course in Uzhhorod. She worked in a store and then managed to reach Uzhhorod and later Budapest where she was arrested and send to Sipa Riga camp or Bocce camp (reference is to the Backa camp near the Yugoslav border)[4]. With the rapid advances of the Russian armies she was transported to the Stutthof concentration camp near the port city of Danzig.

```
Name:  GOLDBERGER,  Aranka          Stutth.Häftl.Nr.  68 372
                                    Sch.H.polit.Jd.

geb.
am:  8.4.18  in:  Szobranz              Nat.   ung.

Eingeliefert im KL-Stutthof          Einlieferungsbuch
am   9.8.44                          des KL-Stutthof

von  Sipo Riga

Bemerkung:    _

                                        OCC 25/14

                                     Ordner Nr.  34

                                     Seite:    35
```

Aranka's residence card after the war

Aranka Goldberger was born in Sobrance, April 8, 1918. She arrived from the Sipa Riga camp to the Stutthof concentration camp on August 9, 1944. See her camp card.

Aranka claims she was in Auschwitz but the next sentence she speaks of East Prussia which is where Stutthof was located. The camp was soon evacuated for the Red armies are approaching. All inmates are sent on long death marches where many of them perished. Aranka was liberated by the Russian army in East Prussia and headed to Warsaw and then to Sobrance where she found no survivors. She then moved to Uzhhorod where her brother Zdenek Toman found her and took her to his home in Kosice and later to Prague. Aranka worked for the Ministry of Social Welfare and met and married Imre or Imrich Rosenberg,an official of the repatriation commission within the Social Welfare Ministry. They married on October 2, 1945 in accordance with Jewish law. She was arrested on April 28th 1948, a day after her brother Zdenek Toman was arrested. She remained in jail until the trial on June 23, 1949. She was accused of dealing in foreign currency, treasonable activities and received 15 years of hard labor. She appealed the sentence on April 3, 1950 but the appeal was rejected. She served 13 years of her sentence and was released from jail. While in prison, her husband Imre Rosenberg divorced her. He married Truda Osterman in Ottawa, Canada.. Aranka finished her jail sentence and was permitted to join her brothers in Venezuela. She later returned to

Czechoslovakia and conducted an active but fruitless search for her nephew. She lived and married in Venezuela. She and her husband established the Eksa company that sold similar items to the Gexim company of her brother. Aranka died on April 21, 1999. Her husband died in Venezuela and was buried at the Jewish cemetery.

Rosenberg Itzhak Imrich/Imre was born May 17, 1913 in Nové Mesto nad Váhom, Slovakia, Slovakia. His father Samuel Moshe known as Maurice was in the furniture business in Nové Mesto. They had two sons: Imre and Avraham known as Adulo. Imre finished elementary and high school in Nové Mesto. He was active in the Zionist student movement. studied law at the Bratislava University and held various posts in the Maccabi Hatzair organization in Czechoslovakia. He wrote articles for the Zionist publications in Czechoslovakia. Visited Palestine prior to WWII. He continued his legal studies at the Hague in Holland where he specialized in minority rights. The war found him in England where he joined the Czech Government in Exile. He represented the Czech Jewish interests in the government in exile. He returned with the government to liberated Czechoslovakia and was appointed to the Repatriation Commission. He was later moved to the Ministry of Foreign Affairs. Due to his outspoken Zionist views he had difficulty keeping his governmental posts. He was also very active on behalf of the Jewish community. He married Aranka Goldberger, sister of Zoltan Toman in Prague on October 2, 1945. He left the government and entered the private sector. He had several positions and finally joined a financial company named Joint and Co. He traveled frequently abroad on behalf of the concern and his last trip sent him to Belgium. He was in Brussels when the Communists seized power. He left Belgium and headed to London when the Czech police began to look for him at home. Of course, he remained in England and began frantic efforts to find out what happened to his wife. Information was hard to come by but the situation looked ominous. Then the secret trial took place and his wife received 15 years of hard labor. He, Imrich Rosenberg was condemned in absentia to a life sentence of hard labor and loss of all assets. He decided to head to Canada. He arrived penniless and started odd jobs to keep going. Then he started to deal in real estate and later joined the academic world. He divorced Aranka in 1954 when she was still serving time in prison. He later married Truda Osterman a psychologist. They lived in Israel and then returned to Canada. He died in 1986.

Imrich Itzhak Rosenberg

Imrich Itzhak Rosenberg, Czech Jewish leader and high government official.

Avraham Rosenberg survived the Slovakian camp of Sered and the Theresienstadt concentration camp. He was liberated by the Russians and returned to Nové Mesto. In November of 1949, he and his family left Czechoslovakia for Israel.

Fanny (Franziska) Thoman was born on December 29, 1882 in Sobrance. She was a sister of Rosalia Thoman the wife of David Goldberger in Sobrance. Fanny moved to Germany where she lived in her villa in Berlin.

Fanny Thoman address card in Berlin Dahlen, Kesserstrasse 21

In 1940 she was later moved to Berlin-Charlottenburg, Berliner Strasse 97. In October 1943 she was sent to the Ravensbruck concentration camp with her niece Lenke Goldberger. Fanny Thoman died at the camp on February 5, 1945.

Footnotes

1. Information provided by Cecilia Goldberger, daughter in law of Armin Goldberger.
2. According to Czech unofficial police report submitted to the court at the trial of Toman.
3. Information provided by D.Gutman, nephew of Zdenek Toman.
4. Biography submitted by Aranka Goldberg-Rosenberg to the court in Prague.

Chapter II
Toman's Background

Street in Sobrance, Slovakia

The village is called Sobranz in German, Szobranc in Hungarian and Sobrance in Slovak; the hamlet is an old historic site located in the eastern part of Slovakia near Kosice and Uzhhorod that is now attached to Ukraine. The city is predominantly Slovak and Catholic. The first recorded presence of a Jew in the hamlet is in 1739. He was a distiller and named Marko Joseffovics. In 1746 another Jew moved into Sobrance by the name of Hersko Abrahamovics. The number of Jews increased with the Austro–Hungarian Empire seizing large parts of Poland notably Galicia. Galician Jews moved to Sobrance in large numbers. In 1780, the "Hevra Kadisha" was established in Sobrance. The synagogue was built in 1800, and by 1875 there were 345 Jews in Sobrance, or 23 % of the local population. The Jewish population grew rapidly and reached about 1500 people between the wars or about 25% of the population[1]. Most of the Jews were small traders, artisans and shopkeepers. The Jewish community was well organized and provided the religious and spiritual needs of the local Jews and those of the district. They also had many voluntary associations, namely a burial society, a relief society and a first aid society. The community of Sobrance was basically orthodox and had a synagogue, a mikvah or ritual bath, a Talmud Torah, a cemetery, and a rabbi. The language of instruction in the Talmud Torah was Hungarian. Following World War One, a Zionist movement emerged led by the Mizrahi or religious Zionist movement. The Aguda or very Orthodox anti–Zionist party dominated Jewish life. There was a sizable following of the Communist ideology amongst the educated Jewish youth. Life in Sobrance continued to flow at a leisurely rural pace and so did Jewish life. Events suddenly reached an explosive point when Germany demanded the Sudeten areas inhabited mostly by Czechs of German descent. Hitler made himself spokesman of the Sudeten residents. First he claimed that they were mistreated and then demanded autonomy for the Sudeten inhabitants[2]. He then demanded total independence for these areas. Hitler's demands knew no bounds.

Of course, Czechoslovakia refused to commit suicide and rejected the German demands. Hitler then threatened military action. England, France and Italy appeased Germany by granting Germany's wishes. On September 30, 1938, these four countries signed an agreement called the "Munich Agreement" whereby Czechoslovakia was forced to surrender the Sudeten areas to Germany. Czechoslovakia was totally bewildered and confused by the behavior of her so-called Allies and friends. Hitler barely digested his new territorial acquisition when he ordered the Wehrmacht or German Army to occupy the rest of Czechoslovakia on March 14, 1939. He was determined to obliterate the state of Czechoslovakia, and divided the country into three small states: the provinces of Moravia and Bohemia formed the Czech State ruled by Emil Hocha under German supervision, a Slovakian state under the leadership of Father Jozef Tiszo and a Carpatho–Ruthenia state in Eastern Czechoslovakia. Sobrance was now in Hungary.

The Hungarians immediately began a policy of harassing local Jews. They started to check Jewish identity papers; non– citizens and people without proper papers were deported to the Ukraine where the Germans killed them. The young Jews were drafted to work battalions where they perished in large numbers on the eastern front. The Hungarians officially closed all Jewish commercial establishments by refusing to issue commercial licenses that were required by every business venture. Jewish professionals were barred from practicing their professions. Hungary slowly adopted all the German anti–Jewish laws and made Jewish life extremely difficult. Then the Germans occupied Hungary. The remaining 321 Jews of Sobrance were rounded up by the Hungarians on March 17, 1944, and sent to the ghetto of Uzhhorod[3]. On May 17, 1944, most of the Jews of Sobrance were sent to Auschwitz–Birkenau death camp where most of them perished including most of the Goldbergers except for Aranka Goldberger and a few others, notably Gisele née Hershkovic Berman and Anna Neufeld.

Asher Goldberger finished elementary school in Sobrance and continued his secondary education in the city of Uzhhorod. He then left for Bratislava where he started to work. He also continued his education at night and received a teacher's certificate. In 1926 he joined the legal Communist Party in Czechoslovakia[6]. He then returned to Sobrance where he devoted his time to political recruitment of members for the party. He was very convincing and managed to attract many young people especially Jews to the party.

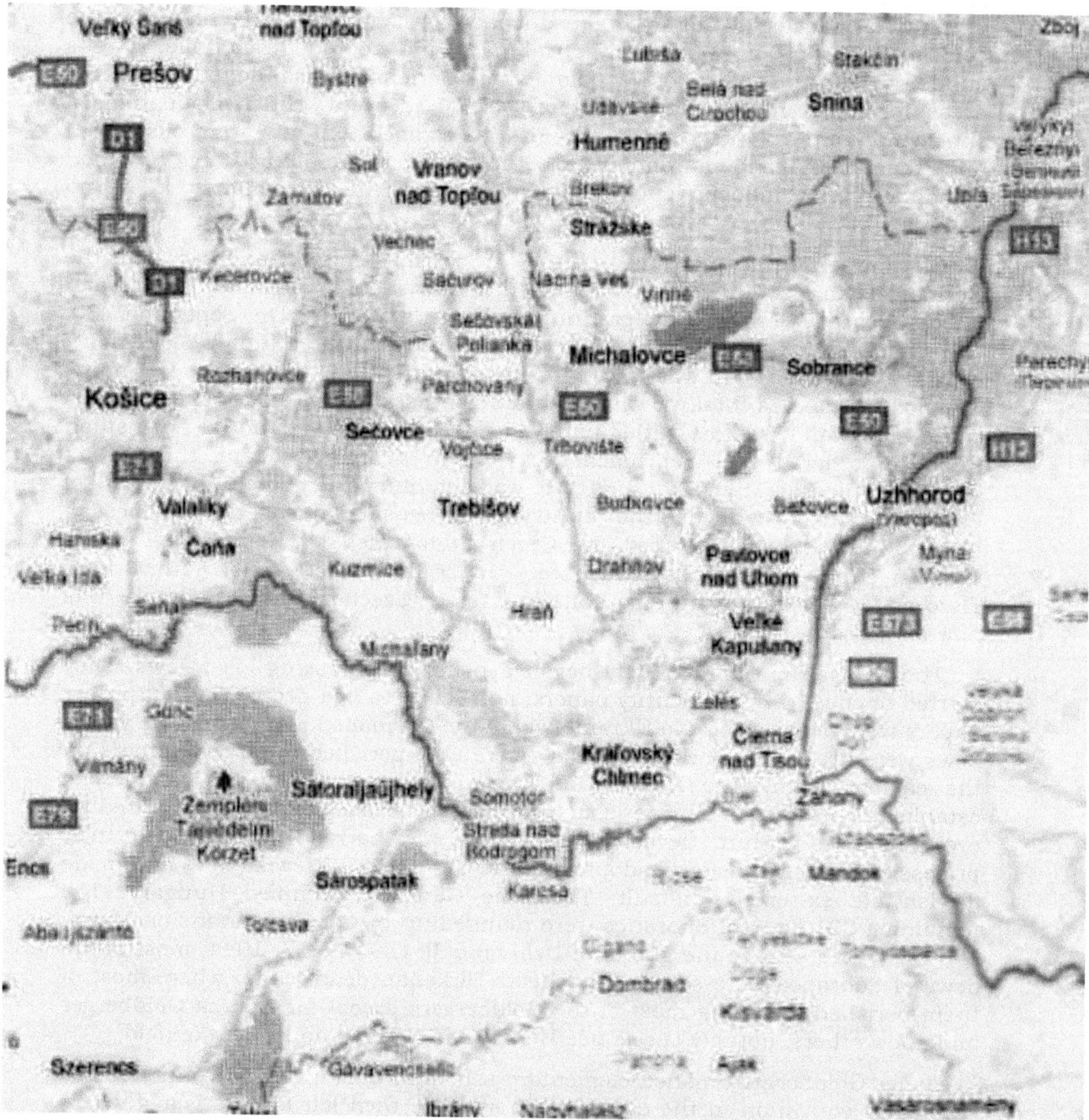

Map of eastern Slovakia with Sobrance marked. The city is east of Presov, Kosice and Michalovce. It is on the border with Ukraine.

After a successful run as a communist organizer and recruiter, Zoltan left Sobrance for Prague with the intention of studying medicine at Charles University[7]. Housing was a problem. He was essentially penniless, in a strange city, and should have qualified for cheaper university–sponsored housing. But Zoltan couldn't dodge his Jewish background. Anti–Semitism kept getting in the way. Zoltan was denied entry into the student dormitories because he was Jewish[8].

Money problems plagued him. Eventually Zoltan was forced to give up his study of medicine since that discipline required attendance at all sessions, every lecture, every class – something Zoltan could not do since he had to work to pay his expenses. Zoltan was forced to a discipline with a more flexible attendance requirement. He found his place in the Faculty of Law where attendance was lax and the overriding requirement was passing the final exams. This elastic attendance prerequisite enabled him to take a teaching position in an outlying village, earning enough money to pay for his studies. While at university Zoltan was active in the student Communist organization and in the youth division of the party[9]. He also began to frequent Communist party headquarters, becoming involved in party politics. Zoltan moved up the ranks, meeting many important leaders of the Czechoslovakian Communist party along the way, like Klement Gottwald, leader of the Czech Communist Party; Rudolf Slansky, secretary of the Czech Communist Party; Vladimir Clementis, an important author; and Vaclav Nosek, Communist labor leader. He also met Pesla Gutman, daughter of Mendel Gutman born in Konske Poland on December 22, 1912. She studied pharmacology at the Charles University of Prague. Asher graduated in 1933 as an attorney[10].

We take liberty in translating and transcribing the circulated secret Czech police biographical sketch of Zdenek Toman after he escaped from the Czech prison in 1948.

Toman Zdenek JUDr   dr. Zoltan Goldberger
Born..........
Slovak Nationality
Former ministerial adviser in the Ministry of Interior
Last address.......
Present address, Caracas, Venezuela
His wife; Pesla née Gutman
Born.......
Son, Ivan
Born....
Zdenek Toman, formerly Zoltan Goldberger is of Jewish origin. He graduated preparatory school in Uzhhorod. He then attended the Karl's University in Prague and graduated in 1933 as a Doctor of Law.

As a student he was very active in the "Komsomol"or Communist Youth Organization from 1926–1936. He was also chairman of the 2nd district of the youth organization in Prague and used the code name of Vasil. During this period he met and married Pesla Gutman in 1936. Following his marriage he worked as an attorney in Slovakia until Germany occupied Czechoslovakia. Being a Jew, he was afraid of the Germans. He managed to get false papers and left the town of Skalica in Slovakia for Berlin where his uncle Thomann lived. He soon left Germany for Poland where he was directed to visit the office of the Czechoslovak Refugee Trust Fund.

The above document was circulated amongst the Czech police forces in pursuit of Toman. Notice the anti–Semitic reference namely that Toman was Jewish. He was also demoted to a mere adviser. No details of the family were included. The document lacked a picture of Toman.

Asher played around with his names until he settled on Zoltan Toman in 1936 according to a CIA secret document[11]. Zoltan was a popular Hungarian first name in Sobrance where many Jewish people spoke Hungarian at home and Slovakian in the street. Toman was derived from his mother's family name of Thomann. Friends called him Zoli for short. The Tomans began to enjoy life and visited the Goldbergers in Sobrance during vacations according to Anna Neufeld, a neighbor of the Goldberger family in Sobrance. The young couple settled in a small provincial city of Skalica near Bratislava. Toman joined a law firm and began to work. The couple began to enjoy life when Hitler decided to dismantle Czechoslovakia. Things changed drastically with the rise of Hitler to power in Germany. We already mentioned that in 1938 Hitler demanded the Sudeten areas along the German border with Czechoslovakia. All sides: France, England, Italy and Germany met in Munich, Germany and on Sept 30, 1938 drafted an agreement whereby Germany received control over the Sudeten areas. Czechoslovakia was not invited to the meeting nor was she asked for her opinion. Britain's Neville Chamberlain, France's Edouard Daladier and Italy's Benito Mussolini signed away Czechoslovakia.

The Sudeten areas were handed over to the Germans. Several months later Hitler ordered the German army to occupy the rest of Czechoslovakia. Hitler broke his own promise and assurances that he would respect Czechoslovakia's independence once he received the Sudeten areas. Czechoslovakia was totally bewildered and confused by the behavior of her so–called allies and friends. But Hitler was determined to obliterate the state of Czechoslovakia; he had barely digested his new territorial acquisition when he ordered the German army to occupy the rest of Czechoslovakia on March 14, 1939. Sobrance was now in Hungary.

Hungary was a pro–Fascist state by the late 1930s. The Kingdom of Hungary relied heavily on trade with Nazi Germany and Mussolini's Fascist Italy to pull Hungary out of depression. In exchange, Germany gave Hungary areas of Czechoslovakia notably in Slovakia. Hungary officially joined the Axis powers in 1940. The Hungarians immediately began apply their anti–Jewish laws in the newly acquired Slovak areas. They started to check Jewish identity papers and used the slightest pretext to expel Jews from the territory by sending them across the border to the German–controlled areas where they were usually killed, notably near the city of Kamenets Podolsky. Hungary adopted all of the crippling German anti–Jewish laws, making life for these former Czech Jews living near the border nearly impossible. Hungary, pressured by Germany, became involved in the war, participating in the invasions of Yugoslavia and the Soviet Union.

The young Hungarian Jews were soon drafted and forced to join labor battalions. It is estimated that about 40,000 young Hungarian Jews were in these formations commanded by rabid anti–Semitic officers and non–commissioned officers. They were sent to the Eastern front and mercilessly treated by their superiors. Only 5,000 survived the war and returned home.

The Communist Party was closed throughout the former Czechoslovakia and the members were being rounded up and arrested, especially the leadership. The Czech political leaders like Eduard Benes, President of Czechoslovakia, resigned following the Munich agreement and left the country. He went to the USA but soon returned to France where he formed the Czech National Liberation Committee. He was soon joined by Jan Masaryk, the son of Thomas Masaryk, father of the Czech Republic. He was followed by many other political figures. Communist leaders like Klement Gottwald and Rudolf Slansky managed to reach Russia while others like Vaclav Nosek and Vladimir Clementis managed to reach England. Pesla Toman was a Polish citizen by birth and returned to Poland. Zdenek Toman could not enter Poland since he was a Czech citizen. He was also a Communist and a Jew and had to hide from the Gestapo. Toman managed to get false identity papers and left Czechoslovakia for Berlin, Germany. He reached the home of his aunt Fanny Thomann. There he was informed that there was a way to reach England[12]. He managed to get a visa to enter Poland where he met his wife. They both went to the Katowice office of the Czech Refugee Trust Fund that helped Czech political refugees to reach Britain. The organization was funded by the British government. The office helped them enter England as domestic workers[13]. The Tomans were employed by Austrian Jewish refugees in England. Zoltan Toman later became a bookkeeper for the Lyons tearoom chain. The Tomans joined the Communist Czech Party in exile in England and became involved in party politics amongst the sizable Czech refugee community in Britain that included Czech military units, which were fighting alongside British troops, notably Czech pilots. Pesla Toman joined the Czech Red Cross organization in England.

The driving force behind the Czech National Liberation Committee was Eduard Benes the former president of Czechoslovakia. The committee comprised many Czech exiles that represented former Czech political parties who were determined to fight to liberate their occupied homeland. Jan Masaryk, former Czech foreign minister, was ably assisted by Eduard Benes. The committee soon sought refuge in England with the collapse of France. The committee was first located in London and then moved to Aston Abbots in Buckinghamshire. Although England provided a home for the committee it still adhered to the

Munich Agreement that destroyed the Czech state. On July 7, 1940, Britain elevated the status of the committee and in 1942 annulled the Munich Agreement that Hitler never observed. Then Britain recognized the Czech National Liberation Committee as the Czech provisional government in exile. The USA and Russia also recognized the Czech government. The Czech provisional government maintained friendly relations with the Soviet Union where there were large Czech military formations led by General Ludwig Swoboda who fought alongside the Russian armies One of his assistants was Bedrich Reicin formerly Reinzinger. He would be shot in 1952. Some Czechoslovak leading communists were in Russia, notably Gottwald and Slansky. The Czech Communist Party was invited to join the government–in–exile following an agreement with Russia in 1943. Vaclav Nosek was named Minister of Interior of the government–in–exile. The latter appointed Zoltan Toman to head the Czech repatriation office[14]. This position was attached to the British Welfare Ministry. The bureau prepared the repatriation of Czech refugees to their homeland and essentially established the infrastructure of liberated Czechoslovakia. Toman placed many Czech communists within the right places of the future administration of Free Czechoslovakia. Toman did an excellent job and became very popular amongst the Czech exile community.

The Soviet armies advanced rapidly throughout Eastern Europe towards the beginning of 1944 and soon approached the 1937 borders of Czechoslovakia. The Czech government–in–exile in London began preparations to move to the liberated areas. Vaclav Nosek then appointed Toman to organize and head military intelligence in the Ministry of Interior[15] in addition to his post as head of the repatriation commission of Czechoslovakia[16]. All Czech ministers flew to Russia in anticipation of entering their liberated homeland. Amongst them was Toman who met Gottwald in Russia. The actual prime minister was Zdenek Freilinger, a left wing social democrat[17]. Gottwald was promoted by Benes to the position of deputy prime minister. Gottwald told Toman that Stalin decided that he (Toman) will be the head of the security forces in liberated Czechoslovakia[18]. According to Professor and later member of the Israeli parliament, Avishay Braverman, Zoltan Toman told him that he met Stalin.[19] The Author Tad Szulc alludes to this meeting having taken place[20]. The meeting must have been one of the highlights in the life of Zoltan Toman to meet face to face the leader of world Communism. It certainly made an impression on the Czech leadership. Toman was one of the first to enter the liberated city of Kosice with the Russian liberating troops. The city was freed in March of 1944. He immediately began to organize the security forces and the workers' militia units. His security apparatus followed the Russian and Czech armies as they advanced throughout the country. The city of Prague revolted prior to the arrival of the Russian forces[21]. The German forces left the city and the Russians were received as heroes.

Meeting of the Czechoslovak Central Committee of the Communist Party
Toman is seated in the second row, second from left

On May 25, 1945, Vaclav Nosek, Czech Minister of the Interior created a secret service organization known as Rozvedka[22]. This was the fourth secret service organization in Czechoslovakia. The Rozvedka was supposed to collect foreign intelligence but it soon penetrated every aspect of Czech life. It owed its allegiance to the Czech Communist Party It was headed from its inception by Zdenek Toman[23]. This service will undergo many name changes and will become known as Section VII. The organization would grow and Toman became a very powerful man. According to the CIA, Toman was also a member of the Russian secret service[24]. He officially changed his name to Zdenek Toman; Zoltan was too Hungarian and Hungarians were not popular in Czechoslovakia immediately after the war. The repatriation commission[25] headed by Toman dealt with thousands of refugees who moved through the country. Assembly points, rest places, special trains and border crossings were organized throughout the country to ship home all non–Czechs. Great efforts were also made to return most Czechs to their homes and families within the country and to absorb returning Czechs from labor camps, concentration camps and foreign countries. Many of these returnees were Jewish survivors who headed home but some were already disappointed with their liberated homeland and began to look for new safe places to live[26]. The returning Shoah survivors encountered mostly hostility and felt ill at ease. They soon began to think about new and safe places. Toman being the head of the security and repatriation in

Czechoslovakia, made it possible for the surviving Jews to cross Czechoslovakia to safety. Even Sobrance did not accept the surviving Jews. Sobrance was returned to Czechoslovakia but there were no Jews in town.

A new Jewish community started to function with the help of the Czech Joint Organization. Some of the Jewish survivors of Sobrance returned to the city to seek survivors and rest from their ordeal. Aranka Goldberger, born as Aurelie Goldberger on April 8, 1918 in Sobrance, returned from the death camps but found no survivors. She survived Sipa Riga camp and Stutthof concentration camp[27]. She was liberated by the Russian armies in Eastern Prussia and reached Sobrance but nobody of her family was there. She moved to Uzhhorod where there were a few Jews, to recuperate. Also Gizele Berman returned to Sobrance but soon left it for Uzhhorod for similar reasons. Gisele Berman soon received the sad news that her husband Nicholas Berman survived the Shoah but was gravely ill in a hospital[28]. She began desperately to search for transportation to reach Prague but none was available. She then met Aranka and told her the problem. Aranka informed Gisele that her brother Zdenek Toman was sending a car to bring her to Prague. She offered Gisele a ride that was immediately accepted. The two women drove to the hospital and located Nicholas. He needed medications that the hospital did not have. The medications were obtained with the help of Toman and his sister. Nicholas slowly recovered and the couple settled in the city of Decin in Czechoslovakia near the German border[29]. The city attracted many Jews from the Uzhhorod area that was now Russian territory. Life was pleasant but there were terrible food shortages. Gisele returned to visit Sobrance where Jews from the area moved to the city and established a Jewish community that would reach about 200 members[30]. The great majority of the Jewish survivors were from the surrounding area and not from the city proper according to Anna Neufeld[31]. Most of the Jews left the city in 1949 and settled in Israel. Presently there are no Jews in Sobrance, Slovakia.

A typical round up of Jews in Slovakia prior to their deportation to the gas chambers in Poland

The Czech government in exile installed itself in the liberated Czech capital of Prague. The first act was to change the title of the government to that of the Provisional Czech Government. Several important acts were immediately adopted namely, political parties were permitted to resume their activities, heavy industry was to be nationalized, elections for parliament to be scheduled as soon as feasible, all German residents in Czechoslovakia were to be sent to Germany, all Hungarian citizens in Slovakia were to be sent to Hungary regardless of how long they had lived in Czechoslovakia. The Czech government also passed regulations to help all refugees to reach their former homes. Of course, all Czech citizens including Jewish citizens were invited by President Benes to return home and help rebuild the country and themselves. Masses of liberated people from the labor camps, concentration camps and Displaced Persons camps of Europe availed themselves of these centers where they were fed, rested and provided with transportation home.

Many of these returnees were Jewish Holocaust survivors. But, already, some were quickly disappointed with the cold, hostile, sometimes violent reception they received in their newly liberated homeland, notably in Slovakia where a pogrom took place in Topocany on September 24, 1945. Some Jews had no alternative but to look for a new home in a safe place outside Czechoslovakia where they could finally live in peace[32]. The Czech government did not stop Jews from leaving Slovakian areas and settling in other areas of Czechoslovakia. The Czech government, especially Jan Masaryk and Eduard Benes were very sympathetic to the plight of Jewish survivors in Europe, especially Czech Jews[33]. There was plenty of empty space since the Czech government deported most Czechs of German descent to Germany. The Czech government, primarily the Minister of Interior permitted all Jewish organizations including JDC or the American Joint Distribution Committee that helped feed and maintain the Jewish Holocaust survivors throughout Europe, or HIAS that helped Jews to emigrate to the USA, or ORT that established technical and vocational training centers to provide the Jewish survivors with technical skills. The Vaad Hatzala helped orthodox Jewish survivors and rabbis to maintain their life style. The OSE health organization provided medical help, the Jewish Agency was mainly interested in promoting Zionist ideas among the survivors. The Zionist movements and Zionist youth groups were interested in organizing the survivors into coherent groups that would eventually proceed to Palestine. The Brichah organization helped Jews move closer to Palestine. The Mossad organized the illegal transportation of Jews to Palestine, while the Hagana recruited Jews to fight in Palestine. We listed the major Jewish organizations but there were other smaller groups that began to function in Prague. The city became the center of Jewish activities in Eastern and Central Europe. The Czech secret police was of course aware of all these activities but kept a distance.

The Jewish community building in Prague where most of the Jewish organizations had offices following World War II

Footnotes

1. Larry Price interviewed Anna Neufeld, former resident of Sobrance
2. Ibid.,
3. William Leibner interview with Anna Neufeld
4.
5. According to the biography of Zoltan Toman (Asher Zelig) at the Ben Gurion Unversity of Beer Sheva in Israel.
6. Czech police biographical sheet of Zdenek Toman following his disappearance.
7. Zoltan, Toman. Short biography submitted by Zoltan Toman to Ben Gurion University.
8. Inga Deutchkron, The Anonymous Donor from Caracas Reveals Himself, Maariv newspaper, April 23, 1982. Hebrew
9. Czech police biographical sheet following Zdeneke Toman's disappearance.
10. Secret Czech police biographical sketch of Zdenek Toman after he escaped from Czech prison in 1948
11. Ibid.,
12. Czech police biographical sheet following Zdeneke Toman's disappearance.
13. Szulc, Alliance, p.144
14. Inga Deutchkron: The Anonymous Donor from Caracas Reveals Himself, Maariv newspaper, April 23, 1982. Hebrew
15. Toman file published by the office of the investigation of crimes committed under the Communist regime.
16. Czech official biography of Dr. Zoltan Toman
17. Szulc Alliance p141
18. Szulc Alliance p143
19. Professor Avishay Braverman head of Ben Gurion University was invited by Toman to his home in Caracas where they had long conversations. Braverman gave an interview to Larry Price regarding Toman.
20. Tad Szulc, Alliance, p.145
21. On May 5th, 1945, the city of Prague revolted. The rebels seized the radio station that called the Czechs to action. Barricades went up all over the city that stopped traffic. The fighting with the German isolated posts inside the city went on for a few days. At a critical moment of the military situation, the so called Vlassov Army (former Russian soldiers incorporated into German army units under the leadership of General Vlassov) attacked German military units. The Vlassov forces then withdrew from the city. The German forces knew the end was near. They signed a cease fire with the Czech rebels that permitted them to withdraw from the city. The next day, the Russians entered the city and the war ended.
22. Lukes Igor, The Czech special services against American intelligence during the cold war 1945–1948, Project Muse, Vol.1., Number 9. Winter 2007. MIT Press.
23. Ibid.,
24. CIA report.

25. Tad Szulc p. 150
26. Yehuda Bauer, Out of the Ashes, (Pergamon Press, 1989 USA), P. 109
27. Larry Price interview with Anna Neufeld, friend of the Goldberger family.
28. Berman, Gizelle, My Third Life, p.95
29. Ibid., p.95
30. Larry. Price interview with Anna Neufeld, friend of the Goldberger family
31. Larry Price interview with Anna Neufeld
32. Yehuda, Bauer, Out of the Ashes, (Pergamon Press, 1989 USA), P. 109
33. The so-called "Benes Decrees" depriving all Czech citizens of German descent of their citizenship. The Sudeten Germans did the same with the Czech citizens in 1938.

Chapter III
The Transit Station Czechoslovakia

With the end of the war, Czechoslovak Jews begin to return to their former homes. In the Slovakian part of Czechoslovakia, the reception was cold and hostile. Anti–Semitism was deeply embedded amongst the population. The Czech areas were more receptive and friendlier to the Jewish survivors, who needed all the help they could get to re–start their lives. The government permitted local Jewish organizations to reopen their doors. The Jewish community was re–established, notably in Prague by Jewish survivors and some Jewish activists like Imre Rosenberg who returned to Czechoslovakia with the return of the Czech Government in Exile to Prague. Even the Jewish community of Sobrance began a revival. The Czech Government in Exile represented the national spectrum of Czech political life. It had the support of the Soviet Union, since the Czech Communists controlled several important ministries, namely the Ministry of Interior headed by Vaclav Nosek that included the secret service headed by Toman. The Czechoslovak Communist Party reorganized itself rapidly since it had pre–war party cadres that were now reactivated. The Soviet Union exercised overall control of Czechoslovakia but let the Czech government administer the country. The Soviet army presence was reduced to a minimum in the country. This differed from all other East European countries where the Soviet Army and secret service were present in large numbers.

Some Czech Holocaust survivors soon experienced terrible nightmares when they were informed that they would be deported to Germany like all other German residents of Czechoslovakia in accordance with the "Benes Decrees"[1]. The decree stated that all Germans of Czech descent would be deported to Germany. The final definition of who was a German was determined by examining the pre–war records of the language census conducted by the Czechoslovak government prior to World War Two. The census asked the Czechoslovak citizens what language they used at home and what was their favorite cultural adherence. Some Jews stated that their language was German and German culture was their milieu. The census classified them as Germans in spite of the fact that they were just liberated from concentration camps with tattoo numbers from Auschwitz– Birkenau. The affected Jews protested to the Jewish community that protested to the Ministry of Interior. Negotiations resulted between the Jewish officials and the Interior Ministry. Even the JDC intervened on behalf of the affected Jewish families. Exceptions were made for Jews but thousands of former Czech residents of German origin were deported. The same problem took place in Slovakia where some Jews had stated that they spoke Hungarian and adhered to Hungarian culture. Here too the Jewish community had to intervene and stop the deportation of Slovak Jewish families, while Slovaks who claimed to use the Hungarian language were deported to

Hungary. The Interior Ministry, especially the secret service headed by Toman controlled the deportations and border crossings. No Jewish family was deported to Germany or Hungary.

The Jewish community in Czechoslovakia needed help to cope with all the social problems following the Holocaust. The AJDC (American Joint Distribution Committee) or JDC or "Joint" for short soon sent a representative, Harold Trobe, to Prague, to open an office. The JDC office opened on September 13, 1945 in the old city of Prague at 7 Josefova Street.

The organization rented warehouses, and trains with food, medicines and clothing began arriving from the Joint warehouses in France. The Czech Interior Ministry granted permits for all these activities. The Joint opened branch offices, opened and supported old age homes, temporary hostels, and provided direct support to the many Holocaust survivors that frequented the Joint offices. Of course, Toman had his men everywhere and knew what was going on but kept a distance. He gave the JDC a free hand in Czechoslovakia and enabled Joseph Schwartz to mount a minor "Marshal Plan" on behalf of Jewish refugees that crossed the country as well as the Jews that stayed in Czechoslovakia.

The JDC was founded in 1914 in New York City by a group of Jewish philanthropists to alleviate the distress of Jewish communities in Europe suffering the onslaught of World War I. The Joint started its activities in 1914 when the American ambassador to Turkey, Henry Morgenthau, Sr., asked the philanthropist Jacob Schiff to raise $50,000 to provide food and medicines for Palestinian Jewry that was cut off from all support sources. The amount was raised and the supplies were shipped. The Joint organization continues to raise money through voluntary contributions to this day, in order to assist Jews in distress. Over the years the JDC became one of the most effective agencies in the world, overtly or covertly helping Jewish communities in need.

Joseph Schwartz was appointed director of the European Joint in 1940, and was director of JDC's overseas operations from 1942–1950. Hundreds of thousands of Jews now in Israel literally owe their lives to him. Ralph Goldman, former head of the JDC, called Schwartz "A real hero." Immediately after the liberation of France, Schwartz re-established his headquarters in Paris and began to organize JDC programs that would help to rebuild life for Europe's 1.4 million surviving Jews. But the American government also turned to Schwartz for assistance. In 1945, Schwartz accompanied Earl Harrison, who had been recruited by President Truman to investigate the conditions of the Jewish displaced person camps in the American zones of Germany and Austria[2]. Their findings and ultimate report resulted in the improvement of living conditions in these camps. The Allied victory offered no guarantee that the tens of thousands of newly liberated Jews would survive to enjoy the fruits of freedom. To stave off mass starvation, JDC marshalled its resources, instituting an ambitious purchasing and shipping program to provide urgent necessities for Holocaust survivors facing critical local shortages. More than 227 million pounds of food, medicine, clothing, and other supplies were shipped to Europe from U.S. ports[3].

Joseph Schwartz, Director of European joint operations. Dressed in a military uniform

By late 1945, 75,000 Jewish survivors of the Nazi horrors had crowded into hastily set up displaced person camps throughout Germany, Austria and Italy. Conditions were terrible, according to William Leibner, a resident of one of the camps[4]. Earl Harrison, Dean of the University of Pennsylvania Law School, asked Schwartz to accompany him on his official tour of the camps. His landmark report called for separate Jewish camps and for United Nations Relief and Rehabilitation Administration (UNRRA) participation in administering them—with JDC's help. In response, Schwartz virtually re–created JDC, putting together a field organization that covered Europe and later North Africa, designing a more proactive operational strategy.

Supplementing the relief supplied by the army, by UNRRA, and by UNRRA's successor agency – the International Refugee Organization or IRO, JDC distributed emergency aid, but also fed the educational and cultural needs of the displaced, providing typewriters, books, Torah scrolls, ritual articles, and holiday provisions. JDC funds were directed at restoring a sense of community and normalcy in the camps with new medical facilities, schools, synagogues, and cultural activities.

Over the next two years, the influx of refugees from all over Central and Eastern Europe would more than triple the number of Jews in the DP camps. Their number included Polish Jews who had returned from their wartime refuge in the Soviet Union only to flee once again westward, from renewed anti–Semitism and the July 1946 Kielce pogrom.

At the same time, JDC was helping sustain tens of thousands of Jews who remained in Eastern Europe, as well as thousands of others living in the West outside the DP camps in Jewish communities also receiving reconstruction assistance from JDC[5].

In 1946, an estimated 120,000 Jews were in Hungary, 65,000 in Poland, and more than half of Romania's 380,000 Jews depended on JDC for food and other basic needs. By 1947, JDC was supporting 380 medical facilities across the continent, and some 137,000 Jewish children were receiving some form of JDC aid. Falling victim to Cold War tensions, the JDC was expelled from Romania, Poland and Bulgaria in 1949, from Czechoslovakia in 1950, and from Hungary in 1953.

Joseph Schwartz was a brilliant and exceptional man. Known as "Packy" to those close to him, he was born in Ukraine and moved to Baltimore at an early age. A distinguished educator and scholar and an authority on Semitics and Semitic literature, Schwartz received his doctorate from Yale, following his graduation from the Rabbi Isaac Elchanan Seminary of Yeshiva University. Schwartz taught at the American University in Cairo and at Long Island University and then served as Director of the Federation of Jewish Charities in Brooklyn. He served the JDC from 1939–1950, and then went on to become the Executive Vice–Chairman of the United Jewish Appeal and later the Vice President of Israel Bonds. Schwartz died in 1975.

With the collapse of France in WWII, Schwartz moved his offices to Lisbon. He also had an office in Istanbul. With the liberation of Paris he returned there and directed all Joint operations in liberated Europe until 1949. Over the years the JDC became one of the most effective agencies in the world overtly or covertly helping Jewish communities in need. Paris was the center office of the European Joint operation that provided food, medical, financial and spiritual needs of the Jewish survivors in liberated Europe. Schwartz was directly responsible to the board of governors of the Joint organization in New York.

The UNRRA (United Nations Relief and Rehabilitation Administration) and the Red Cross were also busy helping the thousands of war refugees that were heading home. They all criss–crossed Czechoslovakia where things began to function and the Administration controlled matters. Huge refugee camps were set up by the Czechs where the refugees rested before their journey back home. Many Jewish Holocaust survivors also took advantage of these facilities on their way to their former homes. The survivors in Western Europe slowly rebuilt their lives and resumed their pre–war activities with some help of the Joint and the local governments. In Eastern Europe, especially Poland, Slovakia, Romania, Hungary and Carpatho–Ruthenia the returning survivors found hostility. The local population despised them and frequently abused them physically; some areas experienced anti–Jewish pogroms notably in Slovakia and Poland[6]. The Jewish survivors began to take inventory of their situation. They were sole survivors of large families surrounded by hostility. They could not stay in their native areas and gravitated to the larger cities, but they were restless and rootless. They sat on their suitcases waiting for something to happen. Some began to journey to Romania hoping to reach Palestine, still others headed back to the camps in Germany and Austria from which most of them had been recently liberated. At first they were individual Jews and later small groups. This decision was highly encouraged by a secret Jewish organization known as the "Brichah"–or escape movement. The organization started in Poland or prewar Polish areas and spread throughout liberated Eastern Europe.

The organization's aim was to evacuate the surviving Jews from Europe and bring them all "home" to Palestine. Most of the Brichah members were young Zionists who had survived the Holocaust. Some were discharged Jewish soldiers from the Polish and Russian armies, others partisans and concentration camp survivors. The Brichah founders and early leaders were Eliezer Lidowsky, Abba Kovner, Shmuel Amarant and Itzhak Tzuckerman[7]. They were Zionist–oriented Holocaust survivors who dreamt of heading to Palestine. But this was much easier said than done. To accomplish their goal, the Brichah leaders began to clandestinely organize in small groups, exploring safe southern routes to Romania, where they hoped to board ships and head to Palestine. The task was arduous and fraught with danger. The Russian security forces were on their trail. The Soviets were not interested in giving Jews the idea that they could leave the growing Soviet Union. Like theater owners the Soviets wanted to keep the theater full with the exit doors sealed.growing Soviet Union. Like theater owners the Soviets wanted to keep the theater full with the exit doors sealed.

The original Brichah group managed to reach Bucharest, the capital of Romania, where the Jewish emissaries had recently arrived from Palestine to help them organize.[8] The hope was that these homeless people would be brought to Palestine where they would find a safe home. These contacts between the Brichah and the Palestinian emissaries in Romania resulted in the establishment of a regular route through some newly acquired Soviet areas as well as through Communist controlled Romania. As the weeks and months went by the stops along this route became more defined and varied in order to elude the Russian police. The numbers of people joining the groups led by Brichah grew exponentially with the increased demand for passage to Palestine.[9] To meet the demand for illegal passage, the Brichah expanded their operations westward into Poland. Krakow, Galicia became the center of operations. The transports left Krakow and headed south to Krosno, Dukla and Nowy Sacz, all located in Galicia, Poland, facing the Czechoslovakian border. According to Salomon or Salek Berger, a native of Krosno

Map of Eastern Europe drawn according to the borders established by the Allied powers in 1945. Notice the Brichah route that starts in Wilno, Lithuania and reaches Czernowitz on the Romanian border and then the Black Sea. Illegal Bricha centers existed in Wilno, Rovno, Lwow and Czernowitz (Cernauti)

It wasn't long before Romania stopped being a way station to Palestine for several reasons: the impossible terrain, the Romanian authorities tightened the border crossings, the Russian secret police took more control of the borders and in Czernowitz even managed to arrest several Bricha groups. A further reason was the shortage of ships, as all Romanian and Bulgarian ships were nationalized by the Communist governments. The most serious problem, however, was what to do with the refugees once they reached Romania? How to get them to Palestine? The Brichah had access to only a few ships willing to risk sailing to Palestine. British government agents had warned ship owners that their vessels would be confiscated and crews jailed if the ships were caught near Palestine.

This made it very difficult for the Brichah to purchase or lease vessels to transport the refugees to Palestine. The situation was exacerbated by the fact that the Brichah continued illegally bringing Jewish refugees into Romania. With no alternative the Brichah began the search for other possible routes to get these Jewish refugees out of Eastern Europe. Such contacts were found in Western Europe, notably in Italy.

Most of Italy was liberated by the British 8th Army under the leadership of Field Marshal Bernard Montgomery. Many of his soldiers were Palestinian Jews. The Jewish community in Palestine had volunteered to fight the Nazis as early as 1940. Over 5,000 Jewish volunteers from Palestine were organized into three infantry battalions. The "Jewish Brigade" was established in late 1944, and was officially named the Jewish Infantry Brigade Group, under the command of a career Jewish army officer, Brigadier Ernest F. Benjamin. The Haganah, the Jewish underground army in Palestine, ordered many Haganah men to volunteer for this brigade. These "volunteers" formed Haganah cells within the brigade, and took orders directly from Haganah headquarters in Palestine.

The Jewish Brigade was deployed in Italy. One of the main Haganah officers in the Jewish Brigade was Captain Aaron Ishai Hooter; another was Sergeant Mordecai Surkiss. As the troops marched through Italy, these two men instructed their Haganah cells to be on the lookout for Italian Jewish survivors. These survivors, seeing the Star of David on the Jewish Brigade soldiers' shoulders, came out of hiding, ragged, hungry, desperate. Hooter and Surkiss helped organize support systems for these survivors, everything from small dispensaries to soup kitchens, all using British supplies and facilities. As mentioned earlier, the Brichah movement was primarily interested in moving the Jews out of Europe to Palestine by any and all means. The Jewish brigade and the Brichah began to work closely together to get Jews to Palestine. These two organizations were soon joined by another organization called the "Mossad".

Shaul Avigur, head of the "Mossad" or illegal aliyah to Palestine

This was a secret organization created by the Jewish Agency and headed by Shaul Avigur. Avigur was born in Russia and brought to Palestine as a child. He devoted himself to military matters and joined the Haganah at an early age. He was given full command of the "Mossad" organization. He selected his agents that were sent to Europe to smuggle Jews to Palestine illegally[11], and established an effective organization that worked with the Brichah, the Joint, and the Jewish Brigade. All of the above groups were very active and cooperated in Italy and throughout Europe.

Mossad representative in Italy Yehuda Arazi

All the listed groups went into high gear with the arrival in Europe of Yehuda Arazi, dressed as a Polish pilot, smuggled first out of Palestine to Egypt, and then Italy. Polish born Arazi had been appointed head of the Mossad and soon had a stream of small boats moving between Italy and Palestine carrying illegal immigrants[12]. The British navy ignored these small boats not knowing they carried refugees and weapons to Palestine and brought Mossad officials, radio operators and communication technicians back to Italy. Soon an effective communication network was established between the Mossad and Brichah offices throughout Europe, notably in Prague in the community building, and of course the main base operated in Palestine[13].

Shimshon Lang in the British uniform

The Mossad and Brichah offices throughout Europe worked hand in hand with each other as well as with the Jewish Brigade, the local JDC offices, the Jewish Agency of Palestine and the various local Zionist groups. As head of the Mossad in Italy, Arazi arranged the arrival of illegal Jewish refugees to Italy and then transferred them to Palestine. From the end of the war until 1947 nearly 50,000 Jewish refugees had entered Italy. Many of these refugees made it to Palestine, while others, who were on boats which were intercepted by the British navy, were sent to British detention camps in Cyprus.

These detentions did not deter Arazi from continuing to send Jewish refugees to Palestine. The Mossad office in Italy greatly expanded its activities. To do so Arazi relied heavily on the Jewish Brigade, and Jewish soldiers in the British Army like Shimshon Lang, one of the 300 drivers in the 462nd General Transport Battalion of the British 8th army.

Lang's story was typical of the Palestinian Jews. Lang had escaped Poland for Palestine in 1939 on an illegal ship[14]. The ship was stopped by the British navy and Lang was given a choice, spend the next few years in an internment camp or join the British Army. He chose the latter, and served until 1945. In an interview, Shimshon Lang said, "My unit delivered supplies to the army units from the coastal areas in Southern Italy, and on the return journey loaded the trucks with refugees[15]. I spoke to the young skeletal survivors in Yiddish and saw myself as one of them that happened to have escaped Hitler's death squad nets just in time. They represented to me the survivors of my family that perished in the Holocaust. No British army rule could stop me from extending help to my surviving brethren. I was not alone with these thoughts, others felt the same way. We translated the ideas into reality by transporting the surviving Jews from Austrian and German D.P. camps to Italy and then to Palestine. We used empty shipping containers or extra military uniforms to hide the refugees at border crossings." According to Lang, not only trucking units were involved in this movement of Jewish refugees. Ambulances and maintenance vehicles were also used to smuggle survivors from the concentration camps in Austria and Germany into Italy. Most of the Jewish volunteers for the British forces in Palestine were similar to Shimon Lang; born in Europe and barely escaped to Palestine.

The war's end found many of these Jewish soldiers stationed at Treviso, near the triangle of Italy, Yugoslavia and Austria. As they received passes to travel through the surrounding countries, they encountered more survivors, and for many, were faced for the first time with the harsh truth of the Nazi horrors in the concentration camps. Some of the soldiers, if they could, smuggled individual survivors to the Brigade camp. There, in Yiddish, these survivors told their tragic tales, shocking their fellow Jews with news of

the Nazi atrocities. The details of the locations of the concentration camps were passed onto the Haganah. Captain Aaron Ishai Hooter and his staff then set out from the British camp in Treviso in search of the survivors in the concentration camps, in Austria and the British sector of Germany. Hooter and his men soon found Jewish survivors at Bergen Belsen, Mauthausen and other liberated concentration camps now D.P. camps run by UNRRA.

Once Hooter and his associates reported back to Arazi that survivors existed in the concentration camps, Arazi notified his home office in Jerusalem. He was then quickly ordered to remove any survivors he could and bring them to Italy. This order was carried out surreptitiously, using British army trucks and transports. Leo Rosner, a Jewish survivor of Mauthausen, said, "We were several hundred Jewish survivors in the camp of Mauthausen with no place to go[16]. Suddenly an army truck appeared with a Star of David marking. At first we did not believe our eyes. We were certain that we were the only Jews left and suddenly we see other Jews and fighting Jews. The truck was immediately surrounded by Jewish survivors; they kissed and hugged the soldiers. They exchanged greetings and stories. Most of the Jewish soldiers spoke Yiddish as well as the survivors, so communication was easily established. A few days later, more Jewish soldiers appeared. About two weeks later, a convoy of trucks arrived near the camp at night and we were instructed to leave the camp one at a time so as not to arouse suspicion. Most of the Jewish survivors left the Mauthausen concentration camp and headed to the large convoy of trucks. Once we were loaded on the trucks, Jewish soldiers placed empty oil barrels and boxes of ammunition to block the view of the inside of the trucks. The soldiers then pulled tarpaulins over the open areas of the trucks. Finally, the order was given to move out. The trucks traveled towards the Italian border for several hours, crossing the border escorted by military police, also from the Jewish Brigade. The convoy ultimately reached the headquarters of the Jewish Brigade in Treviso, Italy[17]. We rested until we were smuggled into the nearby Modene, Italy D. P. camp."[18] This large and complex operation was not Arazi's only activity in Italy on behalf of the Mossad.

Similar operations, rescuing Jews from Austria and Germany, were constantly carried out. Jewish Brigade soldiers provided the backbone of these operations aided by Jewish partisans and discharged Jewish soldiers from the Polish and Russian armies. Large illegal ships with Jewish survivors soon headed to the shores of Palestine. The British applied heavy pressure in Italy to stop the entry of Jews through the northern border and to control the shores to prevent illegal ships from leaving Italy with Jewish refugees. Arazi's Italian operations were widespread with echoes reaching all the way to London.

As a direct result of all these activities, in July 1945, the British Government decided to relocate most of the Jewish Brigade units to Belgium and the Netherlands. However, the rescues continued.

Soon, British agents picked up the news that a large convoy of Jewish refugees would be heading to the small port of La Spezia in Italy where they were to board two illegal ships, the *Fede* and the *Fenice* heading to Palestine. The British purposefully misinformed the Italian police that a large group of Italian fascists would be heading to the La Spezia port to board the ships. The Italians were told the ships would then head for Spain where the supposed Italian fascists could not be touched by Italian justice. Italian police and security forces were rushed to the entrance of the small port city.

On April 4, 1946, a convoy of 38 British army trucks appeared.[19] The Italian police stopped the convoy and began to search the trucks. Most of the drivers were soldiers of the Jewish Brigade, or other Palestinian units within the British army. Two of the Jewish Brigade soldiers, dressed in their military uniforms, stepped forward and surrendered on condition that the waiting Holocaust survivors be permitted to board the ship since they had no other place to stay. The Italian police quickly realized that they had been set up and permitted the Jewish refugees to board the vessels. Immediately, the Jews renamed the ships. The *Fede* was renamed the *Dov Hoz* as 675 Jewish refugees boarded. The *Fenice* was renamed the *Eliyahu Golomb* as 339 refugees came aboard. These two illegal vessels were left moored to the pier, guarded by Italian police.

The next day Josef de Paz presented himself to the police of La Spezia and asked to join the Jewish survivors heading to Palestine. The request was granted. Of course, most of the Mossad and Brichah agents aboard the ships recognized de Paz as the Mossad's Italian chief Yehuda Arazi who immediately took command of the boats. Arazi began to broadcast appeals for help. The appeals were picked up by the Italian press and the news soon made international headlines. The Jewish passengers aboard the two ships went on a hunger strike and threatened to sink the ship if anyone attempted to board the vessel. Meanwhile, embarrassed by the events, the British insisted that the Italians remove the Jews. But the Italians refused. The struggle lasted nearly thirty days, until May 8, 1946 when the Jewish refugees were finally permitted to sail for Palestine.

Unnoticed by the Italians and the British, Arazi managed to slip off the ship before it sailed, disappearing quickly into the Italian countryside. The Jewish Brigade drivers who had been caught by the Italians faced military court proceedings. Shimshon Lang's trucking battalion was dismantled completely and he was shipped back to Palestine. In an audacious move some of the Jewish Brigade soldiers gave their uniforms to illegal Jewish refugees, who were then unknowingly sent to Palestine as part of the British army units. Other Jewish Brigade soldiers who were mustered out of the British army in Europe joined the Mossad or the Brichah and played a vital role helping Jewish refugees reach Palestine.

Arazi's activities in Italy irritated Reuven Resnik, the JDC director in Rome, who insisted on doing everything legally. Basically, Resnik believed that the JDC's only function was to help the local Jewish community re–establish itself. However, history was making new demands of the JDC. Italy had Jewish Italians who had survived the Holocaust, but also now had thousands of illegal Jewish refugees who wanted to go to Palestine. Their number constantly increased. And Italy could only offer these non–Italians temporary residence in UNRRA supported D.P. camps with no permanent solution to their residency problems. Arazi insisted that the JDC not only support the Italian Jewish community but also help Jewish refugees get into and out of Italy, as they moved on their way to Palestine. To accomplish this, Arazi resorted to illegal activities that Resnik could not abide. Arazi used false documents, bribes, and other shady tactics to facilitate the movement of these Jewish refugees. Resnik refused to cooperate. This created tension between the two men, and their organizations. Protests to Arazi were ignored. Arazi turned to the Jewish â€˜powers that be in Palestine' "to get Resnik off my back". In turn, the Jewish Agency pressured the JDC headquarters in New York to remove Resnik from his position in Rome. Even Jewish leaders from the D.P. camps pressured the JDC to remove Resnik.

Resnik tried to ride out the wave of discontent, but the problems grew daily. Soon he was faced with lack of cooperation on many fronts. Even Resnik's assistant, Gaynor Israel Jacobson resigned. Schwartz accepted the resignation and sent Jacobson to Greece to help organize the JDC activities there. The JDC finally eased Resnik out of the Rome office. This enabled JDC European head Schwartz to effectively take over the Rome office and work with the various organizations in Italy to get Jewish survivors to Palestine.

Italy with its long coastal shores and many ports offered an ideal place to hide illegal ships until boarded by the Jewish refugees who were brought from the nearby Italian Jewish D.P. camps. Similar camps also existed in France notably around the port of Marseilles and vicinity. The Brichah, the Mossad, and the Jewish Brigade cooperated in moving Jews to Palestine.

With the availability of ports and ships in the Mediterranean Sea to transport Jews to Palestine, the Brichah and Mossad had a destination for the thousands of Jewish Holocaust survivors that wanted to leave Eastern and Central Europe. They decided to direct the flow of Jews to Czechoslovakia and hence to Germany, Austria and Italy. Czechoslovakia was chosen as a transit place since most Jewish organizations had offices in Prague. Prague was also very sympathetic to the plight of Jews. Furthermore, Czechoslovakia was administrated by a government that controlled the country and had the support of the country. The country was also sympathetic to the plight of Jews.

Footnotes

1. The so–called "Benes Decrees" depriving all Czech citizens of German descent of their citizenship. The Sudeten Germans did the same with the Czech citizens in 1938.
2. Kochavi, Arieh, Post Holocaust Politics, The University of North Carolina Press, USA . P.36
3. Szulc, Alliance p.154
4. Larry Price interview with William Leibner
5. Bauer. Ashes, p.132
6. Bauer, Yehuda, Ashes. The pogrom in Topolcany Slovakia on September 24th 1945 and the pogrom in Krakow, Poland on August 11th 1945. Pogroms and anti–Jewish events continued to spread throughout Poland and reached its zenith with the Kielce pogrom where 42 surviving Jews were killed. P.105
7. Bauer, Ashes p.2.
8. The Palestinian emissaries disguised themselves as journalists. They were Moshe Auerbach, David Tzimend, and Yossef Kelerman.
9. The founders and leaders of Brichah were Eliezer Lidowsky, Abba Kovner, Shmuel Amarant, and Itzhak Tzuckerman.
10. William Leibner interview with Salomon or Salek Berger
11. Zertal, Idit, From Catastrophe to Power: The Holocaust Survivors and the Emergence of Israel, Cambridge Univ. Press 1998. pp.40–49.
12. Szulc, Alliance. Pp.90–91
13. Szulc, Alliance ,p.91
14. William Leibner interview with Shimshon Lang
15. Ibid.,
16. Rosner, Leo The Holocaust Remembered, USA 1998,Pp.97–100
17. Ibid.,
18. Ibid.,
19. Zertal, Holocaust,p.28

Chapter IV
The Human Flood

Jewish Holocaust survivors did not exactly receive a warm welcome when they returned to their former homes in Eastern Europe.

Most of their homes were occupied by other people. In many instances, their homes were destroyed and their businesses shattered. The local population was suspicious, cold and hostile. Most of the survivors did not recognize the former areas where they had lived. Jewish refugees, who had hidden during the war, found themselves knocking at the doors to their old homes only to be met, many times, with a punch in the face. The Polish citizens who answered the door, had occupied these Jewish homes, often using illegal Nazi documents, and now not only refused to acknowledge any Jewish claim to the property, but resented and probably feared the Jews' return. Finding nothing left for them, the returnees milled around the city looking for shelter, food, even a bit of bread.

The burial of the Jewish pogrom victims in Kielce, Poland

During this period, attacks against these Jewish survivors were a daily occurrence. Poland was in the midst of a violent wave of anti-Semitism that bubbled over into the deadly Kielce pogrom that we already mentioned earlier. The Jews in Kielce were accused of killing a Christian child for the blood needed to bake *matzot*, the unleavened bread Jews eat during the Passover holiday. This "blood-libel" was readily accepted by the Polish masses that rampaged through the streets, killing any Jews they found in the city. The mob was joined by members of the Polish police and other Polish security forces, even though these forces all had to be members of the Communist Party in order to get and keep their jobs. Exacerbating this situation were the nationalist forces that tried to bring down the government. They pointed to the few Jews holding cabinet posts like Yaacov Berman, something unheard of in Poland before World War II, as proof that the Jews controlled Poland. These Jews were of course members of the Communist Party therefore all Jews, especially those that returned from the Soviet Union were all Communists. The Polish masses bought these stories that led to minor anti-Jewish incidents throughout Poland and culminated in the Kielce pogrom.

Resentment was rapidly building against the Polish government. For the first time Jews were in positions of influence and power. Many Poles, who had no love for Jews before the war, were now incensed that Jews had high positions in government. Polish Primate Cardinal August Hlond, condemned the murder of the Jews, but he denied the racist nature of these crimes. To Cardinal Hlond, the Kielce pogrom was a reaction against Jewish bureaucrats serving the communist regime. Another Catholic leader, Cardinal Sapieha, reportedly said that the Jews had brought the violence on themselves. The Jews found themselves caught in a political game where the stakes were life and death.

Special military troops were rushed to Kielce from nearby towns to restore order. The fact that the police and security forces had joined the Kielce mob created panic among the Polish Jewish survivors. Once again, men in uniforms were attacking and killing them. Jewish survivors began to question their safety in Poland. This fear spread quickly to other areas of Eastern Europe[1].

The Polish government was aware of the rising anti-Semitism, but was powerless in the countryside where the nationalist forces dominated the area. Poland was approaching chaos as the two sides were fighting for control of Poland. The government of course did not want to appear as supporting Jews and provide ammunition to the nationalists. Worried that the anti-Communists and general Polish population would claim the government was acting on behalf of the Jews, the Government issued assurances, but they had little effect.

Paralyzed, the country rapidly approached a state of complete anarchy. Sympathetic to and understanding of the Jewish plight, the Polish government saw an option that would quell the uprisings and allow the government to survive: let the Jews leave Poland. Even before the Kielce pogrom, Jews had already decided there was nothing for them in war–ravaged Poland. According to Max (Mordechai) Findling, a Holocaust survivor from the shtetl of Nowy Zmigrod, Galicia, Poland, he returned to his native village after the war and did not find any family survivors. He also encountered a great deal of hostility from the local population. He quickly turned around and headed to the Czech border; he soon reached Germany where he was liberated[2].

In 1945, about 5,000 Polish Jews left Poland and crossed illegally to Czechoslovakia and then to Germany, Austria and Italy. Baltic, Ukrainian, Slovak, Hungarian and Romanian Jews joined this ever–growing trickle of illegal Jewish Holocaust survivors that entered Czechoslovakia. Yohanan Cohen, a Palestinian Brichah official in Poland, described for us a typical event along the road. He led a group of Polish Jews through Czechoslovakia[3]. Their papers stated that they were Austrian citizens returning home from captivity. At the Czech town of Moravska–Ostrava the entire group of Jews was arrested and thrown in jail on suspicion of being Austrian Nazis. The Czech chief of police took a dim view of the group and was not particularly well disposed to Austrians or Germans. They were all locked up in jail. No telephones or notes to the outside to inform someone of what happened. Then Cohen ordered someone in the group to play sick. The man was taken to some infirmary where per chance he met a Jewish doctor. He told the doctor the story and begged him to help. Apparently, the doctor informed the Jewish community of the situation, because the next day the head of the community presented himself at the police station and asked to speak to the arrested Jews. They soon convinced him that they were Polish Jews. The next day they received packages of food from the small Jewish community of Ostrava. The community also informed the Joint office in Prague of the situation. The director of the JDC in Prague, Gaynor Jacobson received the news and began to call on his Czechoslovak contacts, notably Toman, to help. The Jews were soon released and on their way out of Czechoslovakia[4].

On another occasion, Cohen crossed the Polish–Czech border with a transport of Polish Jews. They had a collective pass that they were Greek prisoners of war heading home. The Polish border guards ignored the group as did the Czech border guards. "Suddenly a Russian officer attached to the Czech border patrol asked me (Cohen), the leader of the group, to please say something in Greek." I kept my cool and said "*Itgadal veitkadashe shmei rabba*". The officer replied, "Amen". Apparently the officer was Jewish and recognized the Aramaic words that open the "*Kaddish*" prayer for the deceased. The response of the Russian officer was appropriate and showed that he was familiar with the prayer. Of course, the group continued their illegal journey.

Asher Zelig–Zdenek Goldberger Toman

The Polish Brichah used various subterfuges to cross the Polish–Czech border including forged Red Cross passes or concentration camp identification papers that were forged in Krakow, Poland and in other places in Europe[5]. The Czech government was sympathetic to the flight of the Jews from their recently acquired homes. So the transports of illegal Jews rolled across Czechoslovakia. The Czech border police received orders to accept papers without thorough inspection. Even Jews who did not have papers were permitted to enter Czechoslovakia, according to author Tad Szulc. The orders came from Zdenek Toman, the head of the frontier guards of Czechoslovakia.[6]

Yizchak (Antek) Tzuckerman

Following the Kielce pogrom, Polish Jews decided to leave the country by all means. The Polish government ordered Marshal Marian Spychalski, an avowed Communist and now the Polish deputy minister of defense, to conduct secret negotiations with Yitzchak (Antek) Tzuckerman, one of the leaders of the 1943 Warsaw Ghetto uprising and currently an active member of the Central Committee of Polish Jews. The two worked out a secret agreement that was to commence on July 27, 1946, and end about February 1947, and would not be published by either of the parties. The agreement restricted emigration only to Jews, who also were forbidden to take gold, foreign currency or personal papers when they left Poland. All travel arrangements were the responsibility of the Polish Brichah, which would also handle any and all other problems, including medical attention, food and clothing. Neither the Polish government nor any other Polish official were to be involved in this modern exodus. Lastly, Marshal Spychalski verbally informed Tzuckerman that the agreement only applied to the

Polish–Czech border. While Tzuckerman agreed to this last condition, he was distressed. The Brichah had long been making good use of the short but troublesome journey to the Polish–German border crossing at the port city of Szczecin (Stettin). The crossing point was troublesome due to Polish anti-Semitic attacks on Jews, and the Soviets manning checkpoints along this route. The Russians frequently stopped and searched and sometimes arrested the Jewish refugees. They returned them to the Polish authorities where they faced jail. Now the Polish government had told Tzuckerman this shortcut was off limits. While Tzuckerman understood the reasoning – the Poles wanted to keep the Jewish exit story a secret from both the Soviets and the British – he also knew the Russians were aware that Jews were leaving Poland, although not the extraordinary numbers. The British would have been livid, knowing that many of the fleeing Jews would try to sneak through the blockade around Palestine. And the Poles had another reason not to upset the British. When the Polish government fled Warsaw in 1939 in the face of the Nazi invasion, they took the Polish gold reserves with them, depositing them in English banks. And the gold reserves were still in London. England was in no hurry to return the gold and had used pretext after pretext to delay shipping the precious metal home. While the decision to let most of the Polish Jews leave was quickly turning into a matter of survival for the Polish government, the Poles had no intention of giving the British cause to keep Polish gold any longer than necessary. The Brichah agreed to funnel the massive exodus across the different border points along the Polish–Czech border, notably the village of Nachod.

The Brichah was also determined to use the Szczecin (Stettin) crossing point whenever the need arose, regardless of the dangers.

Marshal Marian Spychalski (center)

In 1946 alone, the Brichah led nearly 30,000 Polish Jewish refugees across the Szczecin border point. The Brichah had another trick: it mingled Jewish refugees on trains carrying German citizens being deported from German areas that had been given to Poland at the Potsdam Conference held in Berlin from July 17 to August 2, 1945. These trains went from Poland directly into Germany. Once the trains stopped in Germany, the Jews were gathered by the Brichah guides and ushered to one of the DP camps in the American zone. After the agreement with Marshal Spychalski was finalized, Tzuckerman brought the document to the Central Committee of Polish Jews for approval. As usual there was disagreement among the Jewish factions: the Communist and Bundist members vociferously objected to the terms. The Jewish Communists were steadily gaining strength in the Central Committee; their allies and the Bundists were also opposed to Jews leaving Poland despite all the real dangers that the Jews faced there. The Jewish Communists and Bundists were determined to build a socialist utopia even though this option or any option that called for remaining in Poland was rejected by most Jewish survivors. The Polish Jewish Communists continued objecting to Jewish emigration from Poland. They believed in a new socialist society where everyone would be equal, and argued that Jews should stay and help with the historic effort. While the actual number of Jewish Communists was small, they were very vocal, influential, and had the support of the Polish Communist Party. The Jewish faction of the communist committee members took the matter all the way up to the office of the Polish Central Committee of the Communist Party. Much to the dismay of these Jewish Communists, they were informed that the top officials of the Communist Party agreed with the terms struck between Spychalski and Tzuckerman.

The Village of Nachod on the Czech side of the Czech–Polish border

After that, the Jewish Communists raised no more objections. The Bund had been one of the largest and best organized Jewish workers' organizations in pre-war Poland. Marxist–Socialist in ideology, the Bund was anchored in a firm belief in a Yiddish–speaking cultural autonomy. Vehemently opposed to Zionism, the Bund demanded that Jews fight for their rights where they lived and continued to adhere to this view even after the war. But when the Spychalski–Tzuckerman agreement was brought for a vote at the Central Committee of the Polish Jews, the Bund members were outvoted. Now the question of funding became crucial. The Brichah appealed to the Polish branch of the JDC to finance the legal transport of thousands of Jews out of Poland.

William Bein, head of the JDC office in Warsaw, was already paying the Brichah's expenses to illegally sneak Jews out of Poland. By the time of the Spychalski–Tzuckerman agreement, thousands of Jews had already crossed the Czech–Polish borders: 5,000 in 1945 alone and that number was dwarfed by the number of immigrants crossing in 1946. Bein informed Dr. Joseph Schwartz, JDC Head in Paris, of the rapid increase in refugees illegally leaving Poland, now mostly across the Czech border. Schwartz answered by sending massive shipments of food, clothing and medical supplies to transit camps in Czechoslovakia where the Polish Jewish refugees stopped briefly on their way to the DP camps in Germany and Austria. The reception camps along the Czech borders were enlarged and stocked with provisions for the Jews arriving from Poland. In May 1945, the total Jewish population in post–war Poland was 42,662. By July 1946, with the massive arrival of repatriated Polish Jews from the Soviet Union, the number swelled to 240,489.

Polish Jews crossing the Polish–Czech border during the winter while Czech and Polish border guards are exchanging some friendly words.

Following the terrifying events in Kielce, the Jews already in Poland and those refugees steadily arriving from the Soviet Union needed little urging to leave. According to Cohen, 32,772 Jews illegally left Poland in August 1946, and 11,101 Jews crossed the Polish–Czech border in September.[7] The fear of another pogrom, a frivolous change of government policy toward the Jews, or a crackdown at the borders was always a dark cloud lurking in the Jews' minds. No Jew wanted to take a chance, especially after what they'd endured during the Holocaust.

Thousands of Polish Jews crossed the Polish–Czech borders at Kladzko, Walbrzych, Katowice, Krosno and Nowy Sacz. The Association of Polish Jewish Religious Communities actively encouraged Jews to leave Poland. Chief Jewish Chaplain of the Polish Army, Colonel Rabbi David Kahane, who was also the head of the Union of Rabbis in liberated Poland, urged all Polish rabbis to help the Polish Jews crossing the Polish–Czech borders.

Polish Jews crossing the Polish–Czech border in broad daylight.

Polish border guard officers with Polish officials.

Gaynor Israel Jacobson, JDC director in Prague

The Joint offices in Czechoslovakia and in Poland were placed on a military

footing to cope with the impending mass movements. The Brichah mobilized all its forces to deal with the transports. Jews crossed the Polish–Czech borders prior to this agreement but the numbers were relatively small.

Joseph Schwartz saw the steady growth of the illegal border crossings and decided to call on Gaynor Israel Jacobson who was on vacation in the USA, recuperating from a serious disease he contracted in Greece. Jacobson accepted the post of JDC director in Prague and arrived in Prague in April 1946[8].

Jacobson began to enlarge the transit facilities and the supply stocks of the Joint Organization in Czechoslovakia. He also met with the Brichah Mossad officials in Prague who had their offices in the same building as the Joint[9].

Jacobson then began to make the rounds of the Czech capital. He met Masaryk and thanked him profusely for the help that Czechoslovakia was extending to the Polish Jewish refugees in transit through Czechoslovakia. He also thanked him for the assistance that the Czech government extended to the various Jewish social agencies that dealt with the Czech Jewish survivors. Masaryk told Jacobson that he must meet Zdenek Toman regarding Jewish matters. Jacobson did not know that Toman was Jewish; very few people in Czechoslovakia knew this fact. According to Tad Szulc, Masaryk even called

Toman to tell him that Jacobson will visit him[10]. Toman received Jacobson in his office. Jacobson began to explain the Jewish situation in Europe and especially in Czechoslovakia. The two men hit it off – both came from similar backgrounds although different countries: Toman grew up in poor and anti–Semitic Slovakia and Jacobson grew up in New York State where he faced a hostile anti–Jewish environment.

Transport of Polish Jews leaving Nachod camp on their way to the Austrian or German D.P. camps

Israel Gaynor Jacobson was born May 12 1892 in Buffalo New York. He reversed his first and middle names so that he was known as Gaynor Israel Jacobson. Gaynor stands for the Hebrew words Gan Or – garden of light. He was very experienced in social work and joined the Joint organization in 1944. Schwartz soon sent him to Italy to handle the special refugee problems there. We already described Jacobson's activities in Italy; he spoke several languages, notably Hebrew and Yiddish.

Toman promised to help Jacobson fulfill his task and assured him that Polish Jewish refugees would continue to cross Czechoslovakia as long as he was chief of security[11]. Jacobson also met Klement Gottwald leader of the Czech Communist party and future leader of the country, Minister of Interior Vaclav Nosek, Zdenek Toman, Nejedly, Minister of Welfare and Labor, and other Czech ministers. The Czech government was well disposed to the plight of East European Jews and was willing to help the Jewish refugees.

Jacobson did not have to wait too long for the avalanche of Jewish refugees pouring into Czechoslovakia. In May of 1946, 3052 Polish Jews crossed illegally to Czechoslovakia, in June of 1946, 8,000, in July of 1946, 19,000. August 1946, 35,346, in September 1946, 12,379 Jews crossed the border illegally[12]. During five months 77,777 Polish Jews crossed the Czech–Polish border at a single place called Nachod. The temporary refugee camp of Nachod could handle about 1000 refugees for a brief period of time. Of course, there were other crossing points along the Czech–Polish borders namely at Broumov and at Szczecin along the Polish–German border.

The number of Polish Jews leaving Poland was staggering in relationship to the total number of Jews following World War II. Of course, Polish Jews kept returning to Poland from Russia and soon joined the Brichah transports. All of these Jews poured into Czechoslovakia illegally through various Polish border points namely Krosno, Dukla, Nowy Sacz, Katowice, Walbrzych (Wadenburg). Polish Jews also moved through the Szczecin area to Berlin, East Germany and then crossed to the American zone in Berlin. We must also remember that Polish Jews left Poland legally to various Western countries and the USA.

Children's transport arrives at Nachod camp.

On occasions there were temporary closures of the border and this resulted in pure chaos until the borders were reopened. Here is a description of the arrival of Polish Jewish refugees to Nachod as described by a JTA correspondent:[13] "All night long. Every night, little groups of Jewish refugees stream across the Polish border into the little town known as Nachod in Czechoslovakia; sometimes their clothes are wet up to their waist, their eyes red and bloated from the strain of trying to see through the darkness, their backs bent." The same author writes, "The Czech–Polish border was reopened last night after being closed for three days. Additional trains have been placed on the Nachod–Bratislava run to speed movements of the Jewish refugees."

According to Jacobson, the Czechs had a de facto arrangement, whereby a committee representing the Welfare and Labor Ministry, the Foreign Affairs Ministry and the Interior Ministry in conjunction with the Czech Joint and local Czech Jewish representatives handled the transient Polish Jewish refugees that crossed into Czechoslovakia[14]. But the number of refugees increased rapidly and so did the expenses. According to Jacobson, the Czech government had already spent 21.000.000 Czech korunas ($420.000) from January 5th 1946 to the beginning of July 1946[15] on food alone, when the Jewish exodus from Eastern Europe had just begun. The Czechs hoped that UNRRA (United Nations Relief and Rehabilitation Administration) would assume some of these costs and the preliminary belief was that Jacobson's organization would pay some of the costs[16]. Czechoslovakia continued to provide food and transportation according to Tad Szulc. The bills were presented to the UNRRA Organization that was supposed to reimburse the Czech government for most of these expenses. The UNRRA however took their time in disbursing the bills;

meanwhile they accumulated. But the borders were kept open and trains picked up the refugees and transported them across the country on orders of Zdenek Toman[17].

The Polish Jewish exodus was joined by thousands of Baltic and Romanian Jews. These Jews were not really Romanian but Polish whom the Brichah had smuggled from Poland to Romania following the war, in the hope that they would sail to Palestine. Few managed to reach the shores of Palestine as we mentioned earlier. The Brichah now smuggled these Jews back to Poland and onward to Czechoslovakia. Many Polish Jewish survivors from Eastern Galicia that was part of Poland and was now part of the Soviet Union refused to stay within the new borders. They slowly filtered back to Poland and headed to the Czech borders.

Another special and delicate problem presented was the Sub Carpathian Jews. The area belonged to Czechoslovakia prior to WWII. Following the war, the Soviets decided to attach the area to the Ukraine. The Russians permitted the Czechs and Slovaks to leave the area and move to Czechoslovakia proper. Most of the population was native to the area and therefore presently Soviet citizens including the Jewish residents that were born in Uzhhorod. So the Jews had to stay in the Soviet Union unless papers were provided that proved that they were Czech or Slovak citizens. Toman and Jacobson played a very careful and dangerous game but managed to get most of these Jews out of these areas and into Czechoslovakia, whereupon most of them left the country under Brichah guidance. It is estimated that about 6000–10000 Jews were involved[18]. Toman was deeply involved in these operations and managed to save thousands of Jews like the Berman family. The Bermans survived the Holocaust and settled in Dĕĕcin in Czechoslovakia. Nicholas Berman was born in Uzhhorod, and was therefore a Soviet citizen while Gisele Berman was born in Sobrance, thus a Czechoslovak citizen. She returned to Sobrance and saw a Jewish community slowly rebuilding itself under the leadership of Dr. Hershkovic. On a given day, the Bermans received an invitation to visit Toman's office in Prague. Although the Bermans knew the Goldbergs, the invitation sent chills down their backs. The name of Toman was feared throughout Czechoslovakia. Toman received the Bermans and told them that they must leave Czechoslovakia if they want to live. According to Toman, the Russian secret police would soon begin to round up all Soviet citizens in Czechoslovakia and deport them to the Soviet Union. Toman further stated that in case of arrest he would not be able to protect the Bermans, and urged them to leave the country immediately. They started to look for relatives in the USA who could send them papers. The Bermans also informed other Jews of the news and they too began to make plans for a hasty departure. Needless to add, Toman informed Jacobson of the impending Soviet police action. The Soviet secret police soon visited the JDC offices in Czechoslovakia but did not find too much. The entire operation produced slim pickings.

The Bermans managed to reach the USA where they were successful. Other Jews from the affected areas managed to reach the USA, Britain and the D.P.

camps in Germany and Austria. The Soviet police knew that somebody leaked the information but they could not prove it.

Another serious problem arose with the arrival of large groups of orthodox and even Hasidic Jews to Prague[19]. Their attire made them visible in Prague that was off limits to Jewish refugees in transit, for the Czech government did not want to officially publicize these activities. It also did not want to antagonize the British and Americans. Most Jewish refugees crossed Czechoslovakia and reached German or Austrian D.P. camps. The Agudath Israel and the Vaad Hatzala organizations, created by orthodox American rabbis to support orthodox rabbis and yeshiva students, organized transports of Jews and sent them to Prague where they hoped to get visas to the USA. These visas were not often issued; meanwhile the Jews became noticeable in the streets of Prague. The Czech government began to pressure the JDC to move the refugees out of the city. Toman pressured Jacobson to do something. The JDC, the Brichah and the Mossad had their hands full with the orthodox refugees who refused to leave the city. Meanwhile the JDC maintained them. Finally, they consented to move under pressure since the JDC and other organs were told that they must go or Czechoslovakia would close the gates. JDC social workers namely Florence Jacobson, Gaynor's wife, began to explain the seriousness of the situation to the various Hasidic factions, notably the possibility that the Czech government would close the borders and they would be stuck in the country. The orthodox Jews began to cooperate with the Joint and some obtained visas to the USA; others moved to France and still others went to D.P. camps in Germany and Austria.[20]

Jewish children arrive in Prague

Footnotes

1. Szulc, alliance, p.151.
2. William Leibner interview with Max Findling
3. Yohanan Cohen, Brichah–Poland report at Yad Vashem, Jerusalem
4. Cohen, Brichah–Poland
5. Bauer. Yehuda The Brichah, published by Athenoun, New York 1970
6. Szulc. Alliance.p. 146
7. Cohen, Brichah report
8. Szulc, Alliance, p. 131
9. Jozefova street number 7, old city of Prague.
10. Martin Smok– movie entitled "Brichah". Toman confirms in an interview that he received such a call from Masaryk.
11. Szulc , Alliance p.143
12. Bauer Yehuda, Brichah.Random House. New York 1970, p.204
13. See letter of Dorothy Greene, a Joint social worker at Nachod Czechoslovakia, dated August 14th 1946.
14. See Jacobson report from Prague to Paris dated 26 July 1946.
15. Ibid
16. Bauer, Ashes, pp.107–108
17. Szulc, Alliance, p. 141
18. Szulc, Aliance,p. 150
19. Szulc, Alliance,p. 163
20. Szulc, Alliance p. 164

Chapter V
The Children's Transport

Rabbi Itzhak Eisik Halevi Herzog, Chief Rabbi of Mandate Palestine

On Friday afternoon, August 23, 1946, the telephone at the JDC in Prague rang. Rabbi Itzhak Eisik Halevi Herzog, Chief Rabbi of Palestine was on the phone pleading for help. The rabbi had decided to leave the UNRRA train that was heading to Prague and then to Paris, France at Moravska–Ostrava. The Sabbath was approaching and he did not want to commit a serious religious sin by traveling on the Sabbath. Originally the train was supposed to be in Prague on this Friday but due to a multitude of delays the train barely entered Czechoslovakia on Friday morning, still a long way from Prague. Rabbi Herzog worked very hard to get all the necessary papers and permits to remove a large number of Polish Jewish orphans and yeshiva students from Poland to Palestine. The concept and the planning of the project took every moment of Rabbi Herzog's time and a good part of his help. Constant changes, orders and counter orders were the order of the day. Rabbi Herzog negotiated and pleaded with the French, Belgian, Czech and Polish governments to grant the necessary papers. Slowly and steadily the project advanced. He received a great deal of help from Rabbi Wohlgelernter, Vaad Ha'hatzalah European representative attached to UNRRA. The UNRRA organization devised an entire plan of action that involved a train that would take the children out of Poland.

The plan called for the Polish railway to send a train to Paris to bring back to Poland disabled Polish soldiers in France in accordance with the UNRRA policy of returning refugees back home. The Polish Red Cross assumed full responsibility for the medical aspects of the train transport. The UNRRA's plan was to use the Polish train being sent empty to Paris to transport the children Rabbi Herzog wanted brought out of Poland. The train was to stop in Prague, where the children would get off and be brought to the Deblice transit camp. The children were to wait in Deblice until the renovations on the orphanages in France and Belgium were completed, approximately six weeks, and then travel to France and Belgium using the French and Belgian visas Rabbi Herzog had obtained. On August 19, 1946 UNRRA Prague sent a telegram to UNRRA Warsaw that the train would be available in Lodz on August 21, 1946. And it was.

The long train, consisting of 44 cars, both with compartments holding eight people, and with regular passenger seats set up in rows, began loading children in Lodz, Poland[1]. The train was to proceed to Katowice, near the Czech/Polish border, where the majority of the children who had been assembled from the different orphanages, would board. After all the passengers had boarded, the train would proceed to Prague, Czechoslovakia where it was scheduled to arrive on Friday, August 23, 1946. An UNRRA manifest for what was termed "Plan 750" listed 750 passengers – the Jewish orphans plus escorts. This was the number of children and escorts Rabbi Herzog expected to board the train. Originally permission had been granted for 1,250 passengers. But because of the logistical difficulties, the number was winnowed down to 750. "Plan750" was quite detailed and seemed at first glance to cover any and all eventualities[2].

MINUTES OF CONFERENCE   -   19TH AUGUST, 1946

15.00 Hours.   UNRRA   15 Home Street.

SUBJECT:-   TRANSPORT FROM LODZ TO PRAGUE OF 750
            JEWISH ORPHAN CHILDREN.

PRESENT:- Mr. M. Berger   - Chief, Welfare and Repatriation
                                    Division, UNRRA.

           Rabbi S. Wasserman
           Mrs. Sinek Wanda   P.U.R.
           Mrs. Palmowska Janina   Polish Red Cross
           Mrs. Sternbach Recha
           Rabbi Soloman W. Wohlgelernter
           Mr. C.P. Horr   - Voluntary Liaison Office, UNRRA.
           Miss J. Hof   - Interpreter - UNRRA.

           After some discussion the following was agreed:-

Routine of journey

Wednesday, 21st August. 22.22 hours train leaves Lodz with 100 to
200 children.   The Polish Red Cross will provide the train with
food and with all supplies, including facilities for children under
three.

Thursday, 22nd August. 06.00 arrive Katowice.   Children to be taken
to Children's Home Zabrze for meals, washing etc.,   Ten buses are
being arranged by Rabbi Wohlgelernter, who will check arrangements
on Tuesday and Wednesday.
16.00 hours Children will return to train, together with other
children from Zabrze, Bytom, Katowice and Krakow area.
18.00 hours train to leave Katowice.
19.00 hours (approx) Supper on train.   Polish Red Cross will
provide this food.

Friday, 23rd August. Breakfast on train before arrival at Prague.
Train may be instructed to stop 10 km. before Prague to unload, but
breakfast will be served sufficiently early.

Additional Data.

1.   The train will be composed of 44 coaches of all kinds,
including Red Cross sleeping cars.   There will be 360 beds and
approximately 30 beds in each sleeping coach.   Children if
necessary to sleep two in each bed.   The separation of boys from
girls by ages and sex will be the responsibility of the leaders.

2.   Lists of children by groups of 25 (or less) have been
prepared.   Each group will have a leader who is also an instructor.
These leaders are to have passports for themselves.

3.   Visas for the children will be for each group as listed.
The children will not have individual visas.   This is in accordance
with the wish of the Czechoslovak Government.   Rabbi Wohlgelernter
will be responsible for informing UNRRA Poland of the official
identity numbers of each group visa.

4.   The leaders will travel with their respective groups and
will be responsible for ensuring:-

        (a) the safety of the children

                                        /(b) checking.........

- (b) checking by numbers and names
- (c) feeding of children
- (d) supervision of children's hand baggage.
- (e) obtaining sanitary and medical attention when necessary.

5. The train will be staffed as follows:-

(a) Major Sokol - in charge of technical and operational matters.

(b) Dr. Alfred Kolmanowicz - in charge of medical matters.

He will have assist⁺ ⁿts:-

(i)	3 other d⋯ors	provided by Polish Red Cross.
(ii)	12 nurses	
(iii)	2 doctors	Provided by Jewish organisation.
(iv)	30 leaders	

6. The Polish Red Cross will provide food, water, and all medical supplies, and will prepare and serve all meals on the train.

7. Rabbi Wohlgelernter will make all arrangements for baggage - hand baggage through group leaders. He will arrange marking, collection and loading of baggage. Marking will be either singly or by groups as convenient. He will arrange special transport at Katowice and Prague for conveyance of baggage as well as of children. No sorting of baggage will be done at the stations or train.

8. Rabbi Wohlgelernter will arrange for the leaders to meet Major Sokol in Katowice to receive his instructions.

9. Rabbi Wohlgelernter will make special transport arrangements for children under three at Lodz and Zabrze (Katowice). The Polish Red Cross will provide all facilities and supervision for under threes from Lodz, and will ensure adequate sanitary arrangements for all on the train.

10. Rabbi Wohlgelernter will be responsible for checking lists with special reference to the ages of the children. UNRRA H.Q., will extract from the list the under-threes in order that they may have special attention. He will refer names of any children apparently over 16 to Rabbi Wohlgelernter.

11. Rabbi Wohlgelernter will telephone to UNRRA Prague from Katowice stating the actual numbers of children and of adults on the train.

In order to make a double check a message will be sent by the Czech Repatriation Mission in Katowice to Prague, No.61849 UNRRA. UNRRA Prague will send a representative to the frontier until the departure of the train from Lodz.

12. All messages to Prague in connection with this operation will be sent through UNRRA Warsaw only.

13. For purposes of contact between Warsaw and Katowice the following address in Katowice will be used:- Dr. Schebesta, ulica Koscielna 8, Katowice.

14. UNRRA Warsaw will arrange for a photographer to be at the train for the purposes of UNRRA records and for future publication when considered advisable by UNRRA. Until then no publicity will be given to this operation.

This is the plan prepared by UNRRA to transport the children out of Poland.

The UNRRA document listed the leaders of the various organizations that would be on the train. Among them were Polish government officials like Wanda Siwek of the Polish Repatriation Office. Major Sokol would be in charge of security. Dr. Alfred Kalmanowicz was in charge of the medical issues. The Vaad Ha'hatzalah was represented by Rabbi Simcha Wasserman, Mrs. Rachel Sternbuch, and Rabbi Solomon Wohlgelernter.

UNRRA Prague notifying UNRRA Warsaw that departure would take place on

Wednesday August 23, 1946

The JDC organization in Poland and Czechoslovakia was totally left out of the picture. But there were a few serious flaws in the plan. Because the children would have to stay in Prague for six weeks until their housing arrangements were completed in France, additional train travel arrangements would need to be made to transport the children to France. The organizers hoped that no unforeseen obstacles would arise to prevent the children moving on. Everyone was well aware of the fact that the Czech government was making an exception to the usual limited transient stay of refugees by allowing the children to stay for a six-week stretch. The other problem was that Rabbi Herzog and many of the children were strict in their observance of Orthodox Jewish tradition.

UNRRA Prague notifying UNRRA Warsaw that departure would take place on Wednesday August 23, 1946

Telephone message from UNRRA Prague that papers cleared and the transport can leave on Tuesday but must telephone to inform of train departure. Message for Rabbi Wohlgelernter, Vaad Ha'hatzalah representative with UNRRA headquarters.

Polish Jewish orphan boarding the children's transport

The telephone message set in motion the entire children's transport. Rabbi Kahane's office in Warsaw sent out immediate messages to all the homes for the children to start leaving their orphanages. All children boarding the train in Lodz were told to be at the train station on Wednesday morning, August 21, 1946. The train with all the UNRRA and Polish personnel was already at the station. Security was tight around it. The children began to arrive; Captain Drucker and Rabbi Becker were there to receive them and direct them to their compartments. The train cars were divided between the Mizrahi children that included the children of the Zabrze orphanage and the Aguda children. The former were led by Moshe Einhorn, Yeshayahu Spiner and Meir Weissblum and the latter by Rachel Sternbuch, Vaad Ha'hatzalah representative in Europe. The Vaad Ha'hatzalah Organization was organized by Orthodox rabbis in the USA to help rabbis and yeshiva students. One of the first groups to reach the train was Rachel Sternbuch surrounded by a group of yeshiva boys carrying a Torah scroll with them. They carried the scroll throughout Russia. Other children began to arrive. The commotion at the station is great; children are saying goodbye to their friends and family. The children board their assigned seats and the train starts to roll in the direction of Katowice where it arrived on Thursday morning. The train was parked at the freight terminal of Katowice to insure maximum security. The children from homes in Bytom, Krakow and Zabrze began to arrive and board the rain in Katowice.

The youngest passenger aboard the Herzog train

The children exchanged greetings and stories and waited – amongst them David Danieli formerly Danelski[3]. David (Danielski) Danieli described how he received news at Zabrze that he was leaving Poland: "At the home we always talked and studied about Eretz Yisrael as the place we intended to go. Suddenly, the word spread throughout the orphanage that a sizable group of children and adults would join a big trainload of children led by Rabbi Herzog that would head to Palestine. None of us knew much about Palestine except that it was the home of the Jews. Preparations and meetings began throughout. Children packed their belongings and began to say farewell to those who were staying. The tension was beyond description. We were dressed in our best clothes and issued extra food for the journey. Each of us had one suitcase that contained everything we owned. We were marched to the nearest tram about 30 kilometers from Zabrze. We entered the freight terminal of the Katowice railway station where the Herzog train was standing. We saw many Jewish children." Danieli's story is similar to that of many of the other Jewish orphans who boarded the train. Born David Danielski in 1932 in the town of Rybnik, in the province of Pszczyna, he was the second child of Max, a baker, and Hannah Danielski; their first son Sasha died in 1928. David was always an independent spirit. His family was not religious but he remembers occasionally attending the town's crowded synagogue on Jewish holidays (he spent most of his time playing with other children in the courtyard). When the Germans invaded Poland, the bakery where Max Danielski worked was appropriated. An Aryan assumed control of the bakery but kept Max on as an employee. The Danielskis were forced to move from their spacious, comfortable apartment into a new one–room flat in a poor section of town that had been allotted to the Jews. To make ends meet, David's mother Hannah began to sell off her family's belongings on the street. During one of these market forays she met a willing buyer, Marta Kapitza, a Polish woman who lived across the street, and became her dealer. Marta took the Danielski items and paid Hannah in food she received when trading with farmers in the surrounding villages. One day Max was told by a friendly policeman that a Nazi anti–Jewish "Aktion" was to take place. Max hurriedly contacted a Polish farmer he knew and arranged for his son David to hide there for a short time. David remembered his mother packing a small suitcase for him and sending him alone by train to the station near the farm, where he followed her instructions to the farm. David stayed and worked on the farm until one day he was sent back to Rybnik, his hometown. His parents were gone; a neighbor took him in and he remained with that family the rest of the war.

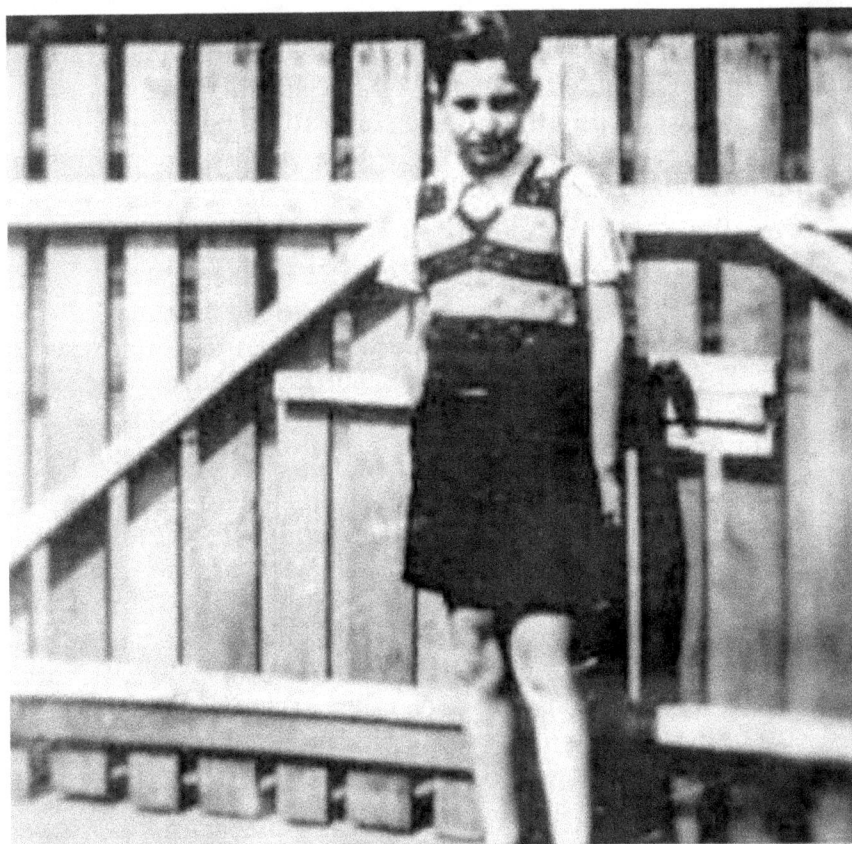

David (Danielski) Danieli at the Zabrze Orphanage, 1946

The train remained standing in Katowice for hours awaiting the arrival of Rabbi Herzog and his entourage. They were still hammering out the agreement that would enable the transport to enter the refugee camp in Prague. At last, the director of UNRRA, Fiorello LaGuardia, granted the permit. Late Thursday evening, Rabbi Herzog headed to the Warsaw airport where he took a plane to Katowice. He boarded the children's transport and it started to roll to the Czech border.

Traveling at about 30 km per hour, the normal speed for Polish trains at the time, it was nearly midnight when the train slowed down as it approached the border. Some of the passengers on the train were stowaways who had snuck on, hoping to get out of Poland without appearing on the passenger lists. This was a tricky proposition fraught with danger. A stowaway could be arrested and imprisoned, with no hope of ever getting the necessary papers to leave Poland. As the train cruised to the Polish border station, one of the stowaways, a teacher from one of the orphanages who had inserted herself in with a group of children, lost her nerve. She must have been growing steadily more frightened with each kilometer the train covered, getting closer and closer to the border. First she moved out of the compartment where she'd been sitting with the children from her orphanage, and then in the corridor slowly made her way toward the door. The children she'd been with, who considered her their foster mother, wouldn't leave her side. When she got up, they got up, when she moved to the door, they moved to the door. She could not convince them to go back to the compartment. Until the fear was too much for her to bear. She yanked open the compartment door and leaped from the moving train. The problem was, some of the children jumped down with her[4].

Polish border guards saw the teacher and the children. The guards sprinted from their posts, surrounding the teacher and children just as the train came to a full stop. Then, once the train had stopped, more students jumped down from the train crying "This is our mother. Our mother died, and now she is our mother. You can't take her away." But the guards did just that while the children cried in protest.

The locomotive was still churning when another unpleasant surprise sprang upon them. Polish border guards, probably because of the stowaway teacher, had boarded the train and were painstakingly checking the documents, car by car, compartment by compartment, of each and every passenger. Even though the children were traveling on group visas, the process seemed to take forever. Minders from the different orphanages had in their hands lists of their children, a body count, and the French and Belgian entry permits. Still, the border guards rifled through the papers, keeping a written tally as they moved slowly from compartment to compartment.

When the guards finished their counting, their commander showed the tally sheet to Major Sobol, the security officer of the train. The latter showed the paper to the rabbi and the UNRRA staff. There were 10 more people on the train than on the travel manifests. The original UNRRA plan for 750 children had been reduced to only 500 accompanied by 101 supervisors. But somehow there were now 111 supervisors. Until the situation was resolved the train was not permitted to clear the border[5].

The rabbi asked for a recount, the guards complied and the tally was the same. The rabbi intervened on behalf of the stowaways but the guard officer was adamant. The people had to be found and removed from the train. The behavior of the officer was a bit strange in view of the order that the Polish government gave to all border posts along the Polish Czech border to ignore the illegal Jewish refugees that were crossing the border to enter Czechoslovakia in accordance with the recently signed Spichalski–Tzuckerman agreement. According to Professor Yehuda Bauer, 33,346 Polish Jews crossed the Czech border in August 1946 on either side of the tracks. Apparently the officer did not like the rabbi or the Jewish children or both. He ordered a full search until the culprits were found. The guards searched for the stowaways until they located 10 women; one the mother of a nine–year old child from one of the orphanages, the others relatives or friends of those legally aboard the train. Screaming and crying for help from the rabbi or anyone who would listen, the women were forcibly removed from the train.

Once the stowaways were removed, the Polish guards gave the conductor permission for the train to continue across the border. Just before the train began to roll, Captain Drucker, Rabbi Becker and the Polish soldiers assigned to escort the children jumped off the train, their jobs completed. Drucker later said that one of the non–Jewish Polish soldiers assigned to escort the train told Drucker he was happy to have had the detail. The soldier admitted to Drucker he was really a Jew, not a gentile, and that his wife and five children had all been murdered by the Nazis. Drucker patted him on the shoulder and then stood near the tracks watching as the train moved beneath the border signs that marked Polish and Czech territory. Drucker waved at the children he'd brought out of the farms, monasteries and convents in the hope they would find a better life where they were going – a life better than the one they'd been handed so far.

The Czech border guards barely glanced at the children's transit visas when the Herzog train crossed the border. The train started to roll towards Prague that was still about twelve hours away. The rabbi knew that the train would never make it to the Czech capital before Sabbath. With each minute the Sabbath was approaching and the train was nowhere near Prague. How could the rabbi permit the train to travel on the Sabbath, one of the iron–clad no–no's of Orthodox Judaism?

Rabbi Herzog decided to speak to the security chief and explain the situation to him. Major Sobol listened to the rabbi and then told him that the train was already behind schedule and he could not let it stand for an extra full day with sick and disabled Poles waiting in Paris for the train to go home to Poland. The major told the rabbi that the train would take him to Prague as agreed. Otherwise, the rabbi could leave the train whenever he wanted. The major informed the rabbi that they were approaching the Czech city of Ostrava.

The rabbi decided to leave the train at the Ostrava rail station. Trusting that the Almighty would smile favorably upon his decision, the rabbi took the risk he could find shelter and food for the 600 children and staff members in a small border town like Ostrava. He instructed all aboard to gather their belongings and leave the train. He made certain the supervisors checked each compartment to make sure no one was left behind. One imagines the rabbi had serious doubts when he stepped off the train. Rabbi Herzog now not only had to find shelter for the Sabbath for his flock but he also had to figure out a way to get them to Prague once the Sabbath was over.

Ostrava, about 290 kilometers from Prague, sits along the merger of the Ostravice, Oder, Lucina and Opava rivers. A coal mining and industrial town, Ostrava was off–limits to Jews under the Hapsburg Empire, until about 1792 when a Jewish distiller arrived and opened up a business. After the Hapsburg Empire granted Jews freedom of movement in 1848, more arrived. The Rothschilds opened a steel mill there in the late 1800s. By 1900 there were about 3,200 Jews in Ostrava, the third largest Czech Jewish population after Prague and Brno. About 7,000 Jews lived in Ostrava before the outbreak of WW II. The Nazis deported approximately 4,000 Jews from Ostrava to Terezin (Theresiensdadt), in Czechoslovakia, the rest to other concentration camps. Ostrava's six synagogues were burned down. The town was badly damaged during the war by Allied bombs aiming at the steel mills. After the war ended about 250 Jews returned to the town.

With nowhere to go, the transport children milled around the railroad station, their minders trying to keep them out of trouble. The rabbi's staff sent frantic cables to the UNRRA offices in Prague and Warsaw, but the offices were already closed. Mrs. Rachel Sternbuch, Vaad Ha'hatztalah representative in Europe, contacted the Vaad Ha'hatzalah office in Prague, but that too was already closed. When the Prague JDC office received an urgent call pleading for help, one of the staff contacted JDC Prague chief Jacobson. Strange as it seems, up until then, according to JDC cables, Jacobson had no knowledge about a train with children heading to Prague[6]. Surprised by the events, but accustomed to surprises in those extraordinary times, emergency measures were quickly implemented. Luckily for Rabbi Herzog and the passengers on his train, the JDC had some experience handling problems in Ostrava. We already mentioned the group of Polish Jews that were arrested in Ostrava with their Brichah leader Yohanan Cohen, although the scale of the transport dwarfed anything the Ostrava small community had ever faced. Jacobson turned to his contacts with the Ostrava Jewish community and to his influential and powerful friend Toman. Time was of the essence for the Sabbath was approaching. Things moved at a dizzy pace. The Moravska Hotel was immediately cleared of all occupants and assigned to the children. A few others were placed in different locations nearby. Food was located for the transport and preparations began to cook the food for the fast–approaching Sabbath. It seemed that the entire security force in Ostrava was placed at the transport's disposal. Only a high official had such authority and such powers to command. A man like Toman could snap his fingers in Prague and people would jump in Ostrava. However they did it, the arrangements for kosher food and housing were quickly made. By the time the Sabbath arrived the children and staff were lodged and fed. No simple deed in a small Czech town following the war. According to David Danieli, a Polish Jewish Holocaust survivor aboard the children's transport, Rabbi Herzog held Sabbath services in the dining room of the hotel[7]. Following the services, whatever kosher food that could be found was brought out for the youngsters and their supervisors. Challah (braided bread) and wine was provided, probably draining the supplies of the local Jewish community and other places in town. David Danieli recalls that in the morning, the rabbi also conducted Sabbath services. The rabbi organized an afternoon study session for the yeshiva students, reasoning that he was, after all, the Chief Rabbi of Mandatory Palestine.

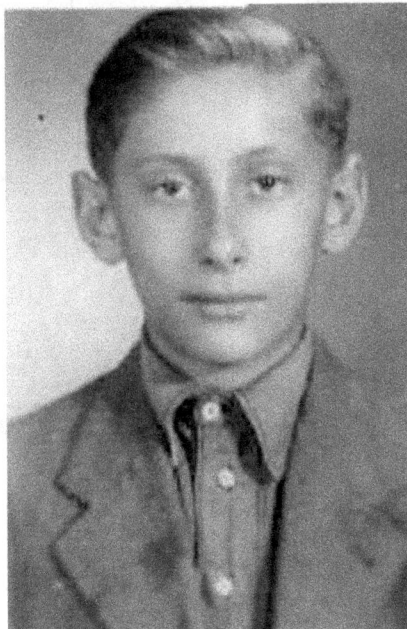

Shlomo Korn

Danieli said that he and many of the other children took the opportunity to explore the town, and then raucously cavort in and around the hotel. According to both Danieli and his friend Shlomo Korn, the hotel was a novelty for most of the Jewish orphans. Most had never been in a hotel nor been exposed to telephones, elevators, carpeted staircases and velvet draperies. Shlomo Korn, another passenger aboard the train, said the hotel was in a pristine condition when they arrived but not when they left[8]. Odd events transpired that Sabbath. An observer reported that during the services one of the girls stood away from the rest of the children, clutching a crucifix, while they prayed. When asked why she hadn't joined the prayers the girl explained that she'd been raised a Catholic and was still not comfortable with being Jewish.

On Sunday morning, the supervisors gathered up the children and shepherded them to the train station where a special train awaited to transport them to Prague. We have to remember that the event took place in 1946 when there were shortages of everything, especially trains. Even the JDC or the Brichah could not provide a passenger train within 24 hours ready to travel to Prague. It had to be somebody important and powerful within the government that could give the right orders and get things done. The only person that had such power was Zoltan Toman. As mentioned earlier, he was the head of the secret police and the border guards, and nobody questioned his orders.

Tumultuous welcome for the children's train at central railway station in Prague

The train ride from Ostrava to Prague was uneventful. On August 25, 1946, the Herzog children's transport train consisting of 500 children and 101 escorts entered the Prague railroad station to a tumultuous welcome organized by the Vaad Ha'hatzalah office in the town. A large banner was unfurled showing the name Vaad Ha'hatzalah. The Prague Vaad Ha'hatzalah was there as were officials were UNRRA officials and Czech officials, journalists, Jewish representatives of the Prague community and some distant relatives of the children. The rabbi addressed the crowd and thanked the Czech government for their hospitality. Some pictures were taken and then the children were taken to the buses that left for the Deblice camp. The Czech government was very sensitive to internal and external pressures and would have preferred less publicity but nobody asked them. The Joint was not invited to the reception and Toman had his men following the scene from a distance.

The 500 youngsters and the 101 escorts quickly boarded buses that took them to the camp officially called Repatriacni Tabor Deblice camp that received only a limited number of illegal Jewish refugees who crossed the Czech border on their way to Germany or Austria. The acceptance of such a large children's transport and for such a long duration was only due to Rabbi Herzog's intensive negotiations with the Czech government and UNRRA. This camp was established by the Czech government to handle the thousands of refugees who crossed Czechoslovakia on their way home. The camp was a former German military base and following WW II, the Czech government handed the camp over to the office of repatriation. This office maintained the camp but UNRRA provided the camp with the basic food and health facilities. Transports of Jewish children had occasionally arrived at the camp from Poland, Romania and Hungary. But the "Herzog Transport" was the largest children's transport that would remain in Prague for a long period of time.

We managed to locate some of the lists of the children that were admitted to the Deblice transit camp. Most of them belonged to the Mizrahi–Hapoel Hamizrahi contingent. The children of the Aguda section have not been located as yet.

Below are lists of children and adults that were admitted to the Deblice camp on August 25, 1946.

Below is a partial list of the Herzog transport in Prague on August 25 1946.

List of children and escorts that were on the train that left Poland on August 21 1946 with Rabbi Herzog the list is only of the children of the Mizrahi group

Last name	First name	Age
AFTERGUT	Nathan	15
AFTERGUT	Sarah	14
AFTERGUT	Roza	12
AGRABSKA	Yanka	13
ALTMAN	Haya	14
ALTMAN	Marina	11
APPELBAUM	Marina	16
ARBETSMAN	Eva	14
ASHKENAZI	Malka	16
ASHKENAZI	Israel	13
ASHKENAZI	Sarah	10
BERGMAN	Itzhak	11
BERGMAN	Eisik	9
BERNSTEIN	Zosha	5
BESSER	Nathan	12
BIRENFELD	Yehiel	15
BIRENFELD	David	11
BLANKENSTEIN	Roman	16
BLASZKOWSKI	Lucian	13
BLAU	Genia	12
BLAUSTEIN	Shimon	16
BLITZ	Yehoshua	
BLUMBERG	David	16
BOKINSKI	Baruch	16
BORENSTEIN	Michal	12
BORGENICHT	Leon	15
BRAMA	Nachman	16
BRAMA	Nachman	14
BRAMA	Nechama	16
BRENDER	Bonek	10
BRENDER	Regina	13
BUCH	Golda	16
DANIELSKI	David	14
DIAMAND	Frida	6
DYM	Berta	12
ENGELHARD	Chaim	15

EPSTEIN	Alexandra	2
FEDERBUSH	Lea	13
FEUR	Hersh	12
FEUR	Lazar	13
FISHER	Lola	15
FISHER	Magozita	12
FISHLER	Leon	13
FLANER	Papa	15
FRAGLAS	Klara	5
FREUND	Risha	14
FREUND	Moshe	14
FRIDLER	Genia	6
FRIDMAN	Irena	15
FRIDMAN	Naphtali	10
FRIDMAN	Rosilia	13
FRIDMAN	David	13
FUTTER	Meche	13
GABER	Solomon	15
GERSHTENBLUT	Zlata	15
GERSHTENBLUT	Rivka	13
GERTNER	Rachel	9
GERTNER	Hinda	9
GESUNTHEIT	Shmuel	12
GETZLER	Markus	15
GINSBURG	Ita	7
GINSBURG	Salomon	3
GLOBINSKA	Rona	15
GOISKI	Yehoshua	12
GOLDBERGER	Harry	15
GOLDFARB	Genia	15
GOTTESDINER	Berek	10
GOTTESDINER	Tzila	8
GOTTESDINER	Sala	4
GREIFNER	Heshek	11
GROMET	Mozed	13
GROMET	Yaakov	13
HENDEL	Hanah	16
HOFFMAN	Helina	12
HOLENBERG	Mania	12
HURT	Esther	16

INDIK	Miriam	11
KAGANOWITZ	Lodziya	8
KAHANA	Lola	13
KANNER	Leon	13
KAPLAN	Eliezer	13
KATZ	Yossef	12
KAWE	Izu	1
KIRSHENBAUM	Sarah	12
KLEIN	Stephan	12
KLEINMAN	Yaakov	15
KLEMPFER	Mendel	16
KLERFALS	Eva	10
KLERFELD	Marian	6
KLODINSKI	Yossef	10
KORZUCH	Fela	12
KORN	Solomon	14
KUPPER	Mark	1
KUPPERBERG	Kazek	10
LANGBERG	Benek	8
LANGBERG	Asher	12
LANGSAM	Frida	15
LANGSAM	Melech	13
LANGSAM	Chana	10
LAUFER	Elimelech	13
LAUFER	Perla	10
LEHRER	Adela	16
LEHRER	Frida	13
LEICHTER	Shoshana	13
LIBERMAN	Nathan	16
LIBERMAN	Dudek	11
LICHT	Charlotta	12
LICHT	Leon	9
LICHTER	Hinda	13
LUFTGLASS	Mashek	14
LUFTGLASS	Esther	10
MANDELBAUM	Rachel	16
MANDELBAUM	Yeshayahu	14
MANDELBAUM	Yossef	15
MANDELBAUM	Gedalia	12
MANDELBAUM	Sarah	12

MANDROWSKI	Israel	16
MANN	Michael	13
MANTIL	Rivka	16
MANTIL	Miriam	14
MANTIL	Haya	11
MAYER	Sonia	14
MAYER	Heniek	12
MEIRSDORF	Sarah	13
MESSERSHMIDT	Mania	14
MIECZIK	Yasha	8
MILSTEIN	Dora	12
MORGENSTERN	Yehoshua	14
MORGENSTERN	Riwka	10
MORGENSTERN	Shoshana	8
MOZES	Nahman	13
NETOWICZ	Celina	12
NEUSTEIN	Elvira	15
NISSANTZWEIG	Eva	11
PCZINEK	Itzhak	13
PETER	Yanek	11
PETER	Dora	8
PINKAS	Melech	13
PRZEDKOWICZ	Ella	15
RAWITZ	Lola	14
RAWITZ	Sabek	14
REISMAN	Esther	11
REIZMAN	Wolff	14
RIGGENHEIM	Hawa	10
ROMMER	Yehuda	9
ROMMER	Berek	15
ROMMER	Fania	13
ROMMER	Mania	12
ROMMER	Esther	9
ROSENBERG	Bluma	9
ROSENBLUM	Monik	13
ROSENBLUM	Rosa	12
ROSENBLUM	Hawa	16
ROSENTHAL	Markus	16
ROSENTHAL	Tzipora	9
ROSENTHAL	Sarah	14

ROTCHILD	Inga	13
RUBINFELD	Blima	12
RUBINSTEIN	Fania	9
RUDESZEWSKI	Moshe	11
RZUBISKI	Aaron	9
RZYPKO	Pessah	14
RZYPKO	Reuven	11
RZYPKO	Zalman	16
SAWITZKI	Yerzy	10
SCHECHTER	Mark	10
SCHECHTER	Tusha	8
SEGALOWICZ	Yeshayahu	14
SHAKRAKA	Motek	14
SHAPIRO	Yehuda	13
SHEFDEL	Chaim	13
SHEIFELD	Basha	14
SZER	Baruch	13
SZER	Golda	15
SHNAYER	Mira	13
SHNAYER	Israel	9
SHOWIN	Henech	13
SHPIGLER	Salek	8
SHPIGLER	Henech	14
SHPILMAN	Karola	8
SHTEINER	Paula	16
SHTEKEL	Yanek	5
SHTURM	Henia	14
SHTURM	Gittel	3
SHTURM	Yehoshua	13
SHUSTER	Roza	1
SHWEITZER	Awraham	10
SOBOL	Heniek	10
SOBOL	Yehuda	14
SONENSHEIN	Rachel	5
SPINER	Miriam	11
STRAUCH	Henia	14
TILLMAN	Nachman	13
TOBIAS	Israel	12
TOTENGRABBER	Ella	14
TREMBLINSKI	Yossef	5

TZENTKIAR	Benjaimin	13
TZUKER	Sonia	4
VERED	Rachel	13
VERED	Felicia	14
WAKSBERG	Yeshayahu	15
WAKSBERG	Israel	14
WASS	Molek	10
WEISBLUM	Aviva	1
WEISSFOGEL	Sabina	15
WEISSMAN	Itzhak	13
WENTZELBERG	Yona	12
WERTHEM	Lila	14
WICZIC	Tusha	15
WIENER	Sala	5
WILNER	Tulek	12
WINBERG	Lipa	7
WINFELD	Wolff	13
WINFELD	Guta	13
WISHNITZER	Leopold	11
WITMAN	Paula	12
WIZENFELD	Danuta	8
WIZENFELD	Arnold	15
WOHLGELERNTER	Palus	5
WURTMAN	Eisik	16
YAAKOV	Tziporah	12
YAAKOV	Shaul	9
ZEIDEN	Elvira	12
ZILBERTZWEIG	Rachel	10
ZILBERTZWEIG	Tula	7
ZOLMAN	Shmuel	13
ZOLMAN	Nathan	9
ZOLMAN	Basha	9
ZRUWANITZER	Hawa	16

Adult Escorts

BIRENFELD	Sarah
EINHORN	Moshe
ENGELHARDT	Dov
ENGELHARDT	Frimta

ERLICH	Awraham
FLOMENBAUM	Benyamin
GABER	Chaim
GABER	Tziporah
GINSBURG	Feie
GINSBURG	Sarah
GLUCHES	Bela
GOLDBERGER	Anna
GOLDBERGER	Yaakow
GOLDBERGER	Haya
GOTTESDINER	Mira
GOTTLIEB	Shimshon
GOTTLIEB	Gisela
KNOBEL	Roza
LUFTGLASS	Sarah
MANDEBAUM	Luba
MANDEBAUM	Duba
RAPPAPORT	Riwka
RICHARD	Mordechai
RICHARD	Dwora
RIMMER	Yente
ROSENGARTEN	Pola
SHAPIRO	Avraham
SHAPIRO	
SHAPIRO	Yehoshua
SHAPIRO	Ella
SHAPIRO	Lea
SHUSTER	Aaron
SHUSTER	Liza
TEPFER	Shalom
WEISSBLUM	Meir
WEISSBLUM	Sarah
WIZENFELD	Mendel
WOHLGELERNTER	Haya
WULKAN	Elimelech
YERED	Sarah
YERED	Lisa
ZOLMAN	Sarah

Foreign Escorts

Rabbi Itzhak Eisik Halevi Herzog
Yaakov Herzog
Rabbi Zeev Gold
Rabbi Itamar Wohlgelernter Vaad Ha'hatzalah Representative
Rachel Sternbuch Vaad Ha'hatzalah Representative
Additional Representatives

The list was found in the Zionist Archives. This is a partial list.

Another partial list of children admitted to the Rapatrianci Dablice Tabor camp in Prague on August 25, 1946. List also found in the Zionist Archives.

ASZER	Nirla	1939
BANDER	Chaya	1930
BINDERMEN	Rifka	1937
BINDERMEN	Josef	1935
BINDERMEN	Chaya	1932
CZERNOGORA	Feiga	1935
CZERNOGORA	Chani	1923
FAYER (FEUER)	Jankel	1933
FAYER (FEUER)	Yankel	1933
FINKELMAN	Liba	1936
FINKELMAN	Chene	1938
FLISZER	Les	1936
FLISZER	Szlama	1931
FOJBOMOIM (FEIGENBOIM)	Pinkusz	1938
FUCHS	Judita	1933
FUCHS	Mojze	1936
GAYER	Mordechai	1930
GAYER	Jankel	1930
GITTELBAUM	Kalmen	1930
GRUBER	Israel	1937
JODWERKER	Ryke	1943
LEHRER	Feige	1936
LEHRER	Izrael	1938
LEHRER	Mayer	1933
LEICHTER	Ruchla	1938
PERL (PEARL)	Arie	1930
RIBAK	Juda	1930
SZIER	Szura	1935
SZIER	Jakub	1931
THERBAUM	Lea	1936
WALTER	Szmul	1938

These are the lists that we located of the children that entered the Deblice camp on August 25 1946.

The UNRRA staff at the camp was well prepared to receive the children and adults. Each group was assigned their place. The group leaders assumed their roles in controlling their children. An overall committee was created of UNRRA, Joint officials, Vaad Ha'hatzalah and Czech welfare officials to supervise the activities of the children.

While the original number of children leaving Poland was to have been 1,000, the number first dropped to 750, and then finally only 500 actually boarded the train. During their stay in the Deblice camp about 12 children were reunited with their families. The JDC had to assume full financial responsibility for the children's welfare in the camp. The six weeks the children stayed in Deblice was a challenge to the children's supervisors and to the JDC. The children's boundless energy had to be channelled or chaos easily ensued. This required both planning and money.

The partial list of children aboard the train. The list is in Hebrew transliterated from a Polish list. The shifting of lists from language to language caused some misspellings and errors of name spelling.

In the Deblice camp, the "madrichim" (counselors) or head counselors and their assistants devised activities for the youngsters. Moshe Einhorn, Yeshua Spiner and Meir Weisblum were in charge of the Mizrahi/Hapoel Hamizrahi contingent. Rachel Sternbuch was in charge of the Aguda contingent. Overall supervision of the children was made up of representatives from UNRRA, the JDC's Czech office, Vaad Ha'hatzalah and the Prague Jewish community. The children had to be kept busy. To do this their supervisors organized cultural and entertaining programs and educational lectures. The Aguda groups devoted their time to study religious materials while the Mizrahi groups devoted their time to educational, historical and cultural activities. David (Danielski) Danieli, who spent much of his childhood hiding out in a Christian home, having no contact with his Jewish brethren, remembers, "We finally left Poland and reached Prague where we remained in this camp for about five weeks. I had never met so many different types of Jews all in one place at the same time".[9]

Jewish orphans with their teacher upon arrival in Prague

The JDC in Prague was totally unprepared for the arrival of the children and their poor condition as can be seen from the pictures. Jacobson sent a cable to headquarters where he states that his office knew nothing about the transport yet when it arrived the Joint office in Prague had to supplement food, buy shoes etc...

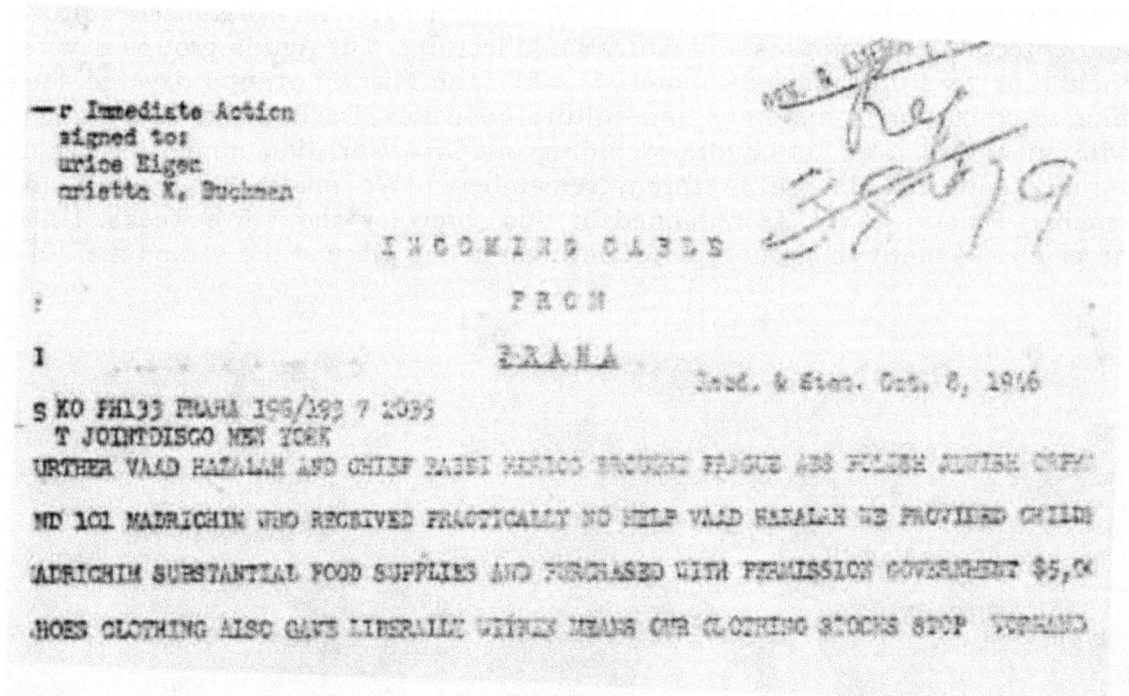

Original cable

Reprinted cable for legibility.

"...FURTHER VAAD HAZALAH AND CHIEF RABBI HERZOG BROUGHT PRAGUE 488 JEWISH ORPHANS AND 101 MADRICHIM WHO RECEIVED PRACTICALLY NO HELP VAAD HAZALAH WE PROVIDED CHILDREN AND MADRICHIM SUBSTANTIAL FOOD SUPPLIES AND PURCHASED WITH PERMISSION GOVERNMENT $5,000 SHOES CLOTHING ALSO GAVE LIBERALLY WITHIN MEANS OUR CLOTHING STORES STOP"

JDC cable # 3879

Telegram sent by Jacobson to JDC headquaters...[10]

"The activities our camp counselors organized kept us busy and before we knew it the High Holidays were on us. The first day of Rosh Hashanah we walked from the camp to the Maharal Synagogue in Prague, the 'Alte Neu Shul.' At the synagogue I heard the story of the 'Golem' for the first time. I was very impressed with the streets of Prague and some of the beautiful buildings. The city was not embarrassed to display Hebrew letters, namely on the bridge or on several buildings. I really enjoyed Prague. When the two–day Rosh Hashanah holiday was over we were told to pack. We were driven to the railway station where we boarded a train"[11]. The train would cross Germany and reach Strasbourg, France where the transport ended the journey for all practical purposes. The Mizrahi contingent including the Zabrze children would leave the train to a tumultuous welcome organized by the Strasbourg Bnei Akiva religious youth group while the Aguda contingent would head to homes in Aix–les–Bains in Southern France.

The Czech government was extremely helpful with the children from the Herzog Train. In a later cable, JDC's Israel Jacobson thanked the Czech government for the enormous help it had provided for all the Jewish refugees, not only the children. Jacobson pointed out that approximately 700 Jewish refugees a day were streaming across the Czech border. No wonder that the JDC was somewhat harried by the sudden appearance of nearly 500 children and another 101 minders. Again, the assistance provided by Zoltan Toman can only be guessed at because no written documents exist.

However, a cable by the JDC's Israel Jacobson to the Czech government points out the many positive press reports that praise the Czech assistance and also hints at Toman's involvement by including his name as a recipient in the cable.

Jewish children aboard the train

AMERICAN JOINT DISTRIBUTION COMMITTEE

PRAHA V. JOSEFOVSKÁ

October 11, 1945

To: AJDC New York - Attention: Mr. Raphael Levy

From: AJDC Prague

Re: Publicity favorable to Czechoslovak Government.

        Officials of the Czech Government are interested in
seeing the kind of publicity Czechoslovakia has received as
a result of its aid to Polish Jews in transit through
Czechoslovakia. Getting from you releases and clippings
favorable to the Czech Government for its actions will not
only be satisfying to them, but will probably be of real
help in planning further cooperative action with the Government.

        Will you kindly arrange to airmail us clippings (prefer-
ably in the English language) as soon as possible.

                                Israel G. Jacobson
                        Director for AJDC Czechoslovakia

IGJ/LB

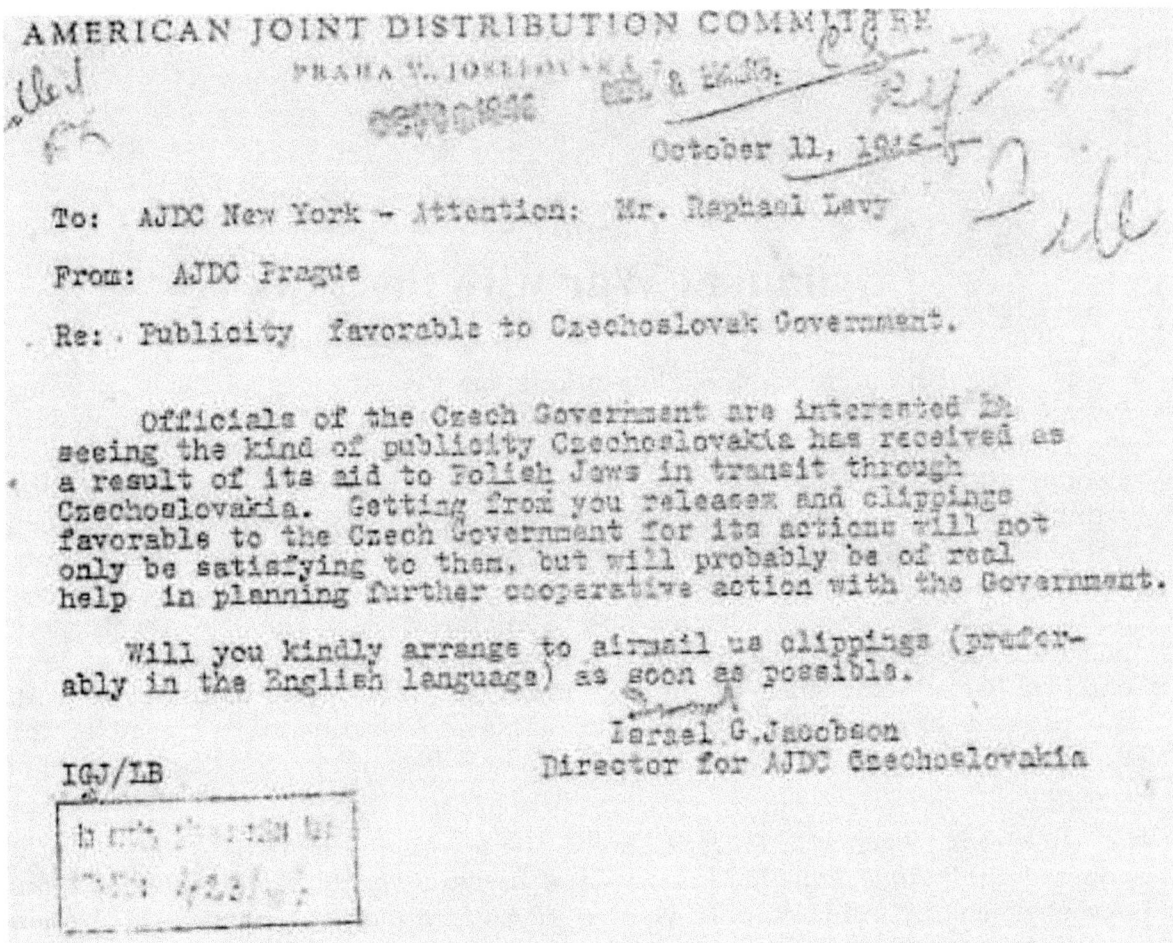

**Publicity letters expressing JDC thanks to the Czech government for the
assistance granted to Jewish refugees crossing Czechoslovakia**

Footnotes

1. Shragai, Rescue, p.72
2. Ibid., p.72
3. William Leibner interview with David Danieli
4. Shragai Report p.85
5. Ibid.,
6. Tad Szulc. Alliance p.164
7. William Leibner interview with David Danieli
8. Ibid.,
9. William Leibner interview with David Danieli
10. Original cable barely legible.
11. William Leibner interview with David Danieli

Chapter VI
Britain at War with the Jews

In 1930 Britain introduced limitations on the number of Jews entering Palestine. From that time, one had to obtain a certificate of entrance granted on the basis of certain qualifications, notably financial or skills. The system was steadily tightened. However, with Hitler's access to power in Germany, the number of Jewish applicants increased each day. In 1936, 60,000 Jews reached the shores of Palestine. The Palestinian Arabs protested and the Arab revolt, which would last until 1939, began. Britain decided to further reduce the number of Jews entering Palestine and to militarily crush the Arab revolt. Both policies succeeded. The Arab revolt was slowly quashed and the number of Jews entering Palestine declined by the day, eventually almost coming to a halt with the passage of the *"White Paper."* The gates of Palestine were closed to the thousands of Jews who would have found a safe haven from the death camps of Europe.

The Jewish Agency of Palestine went along with the British policies until it adopted the *"White Paper"*. This was the breaking point between Britain and Jewish Palestine. Already in 1934, the *"Halutz"* or Zionist pioneer organization in Poland had successfully sent 350 passengers illegally to Palestine on the ship *"Vellos"*.

The Jewish Agency opposed the move and saw to it that such operations were stopped. The *"Vellos"* passengers were helped by the *"Haganah"* or Palestinian Jewish underground as a one–time event. The Revisionist Zionist movement under the leadership of Ze'ev Jabotinsky did not abide by the British rules. It began to organize illegal ships that sailed to Palestine with Jewish passengers. These operations were small due to lack of funds. At first, small boats like *"Af Al Pi"* or *"Dor"* were used but with time, larger vessels like *"Patria"* with 850 passengers in 1939 were used[1]. With the publication of the *"White Paper"* the Jewish Agency created the office called "Mossad l'Aliyah Bet" to handle illegal immigration to Palestine[2]. Illegal ships began to reach Palestine with Jewish immigrants but the British Navy was there to greet them.

The British were well informed of the Jewish situation in Palestine and expected some reactions to their policy of preventing Jews from reaching the country. The Royal Navy was already partially mobilized due to the war–threatening situation in Europe. It received the order to patrol the Mediterranean Sea and intercept illegal ships with Jews. So did the Royal Air

Force. Even the Foreign Office began to apply pressure on Romania to stop the flow of Jews to the Romanian ports where they embarked on boats heading to Palestine.[3] British agents in the Mediterranean ports were ordered to be on the look-out for ships leaving with Jews to Palestine. The British were very successful and stifled the illegal aliyah to Palestine. Some illegal ships still managed to leave Europe but had tragic consequences, notably the "*Patria*" and the "*Struma*". The Patria was blown up by the Haganah on November 25, 1940 to stop it from taking illegal Jewish immigrants to the island of Mauritus. The explosion sunk the boat within minutes and resulted in the estimated death of 267 people[4]. The *Struma* left Romania on December 12, 1941 but barely reached Istanbul, Turkey. The vessel had engine problems. Turkey refused to keep the vessel for repairs, the British refused to grant the passengers certificates, so the Turks hauled the ship out of port where a Russian submarine torpedoed the ship. It is estimated that 781 Jews drowned. There was one survivor.[5] The illegal aliyah stopped, since the organizers refused to take such mortal risks until the end of the war.

With the liberation of Italy from the Germans, the Mossad renewed the illegal shipping of Jewish Holocaust survivors to Palestine. The Royal Navy and Air Force began to chase illegal ships throughout the Mediterranean Sea. They seized most of the ships and sent the passengers to the detention camps on the island of Cyprus. The British armed forces waged a constant struggle with the illegal ships. The British foreign office applied pressure to all the countries notably Italy, France and Greece to stop illegal ships from leaving their ports[6].

With the end of the war, the Jewish Holocaust survivors refused to cooperate with Britain. The hundreds of thousands of Jewish survivors and Jewish refugees who had fled the Nazi horrors and the anti-Semitic pogroms in Eastern Europe were determined to open the gates to Palestine. Most of them had no place to go and only Jewish Palestine wanted them. Britain was determined to keep Palestine closed to Jews. The British armed forces were deployed to prevent Jews from reaching Palestine. Even after the horrible results of WWII became evident, Britain still stubbornly prevented the Jews from entering Palestine, devoting considerable military resources to stop illegal ships carrying Holocaust survivors from landing on the shores of Palestine. Britain already had approximately 50,000 soldiers in Palestine to control the situation and prevent illegal refugees from entering the country. Since 1945 Britain had lost 223 soldiers fighting the Jewish underground in Palestine with 478 wounded in action. These actions did in effect prevent the landing of illegal Jewish refugees on the shores of Palestine but the illegal ships kept coming. Most of them came from Italian ports. The British began to pressure the Italian government to close the borders and to patrol the shores of the Adriatic Sea. The Italian government was happy to see refugees leave the country and did not care to help the British solve their problem, and did not want to take drastic action against Jewish refugees fearing American public opinion. Britain also appealed to France and Greece to prevent illegal ships with Jewish refugees from leaving their ports. All these appeals proved fruitless since the governments of these countries had more pressing problems than chasing Jewish refugees in transit.

The British Foreign Office placed great pressure on European countries notably Poland and especially Czechoslovakia, to prevent Jews from leaving their countries. Britain imposed a blackout on Jewish news in Europe. Even British Jewish social services were prevented from assisting Jewish Holocaust survivors in the British zone of occupied Germany. Rabbi Herzog was not allowed to visit the British zone in Germany. The British foreign minister kept repeating that there is no Jewish problem in Europe therefore no need to discuss Palestine.

Bevin of course admitted that there were refugees in Europe but these were nationals of various European countries notably Poles. "But there were no **Jewish** refugees per se." Bevin urged all refugees, (including the Jewish refugees), to return to their native countries. But England was no longer the Empire that it used to be. Arrayed against it were determined people who survived Hitler. The Holocaust survivors were determined to break the British blockade. They enlisted the help of American public opinion that supported a Jewish homeland in Palestine. This support demanded of President Truman to take action on behalf of the Holocaust refugees. The reasoning was clear; countries, including the USA, did want to admit large numbers of Jewish refugees. Palestine wanted them. Britain refused to budge. It assumed that the USA was just â€˜publicizing' this policy for public consumption. The State Department and the Pentagon assured Britain that the USA would support Britain in the final analysis.' President Truman knew that he had to take a stand and he was in favor of Britain "slightly" opening the gates of Palestine. Immigration to Palestine was becoming an issue between England and the USA. Truman felt that he must give something to his Jewish constituents who were demanding action. The American Jewish soldiers and chaplains wrote home about the terrible conditions of the Jewish Holocaust survivors. These conditions, like keeping them behind wire fencing or German guards policing the camps, became the topic of conversation at Jewish community centers and temples. During the war, the Jewish organizations were promised that that the Jewish situation in Europe would be tended to after the war. They now demanded action. Truman had hoped that Britain would permit some Jews to reach Palestine and thus reduce the pressure, but Britain refused to budge on this issue. Truman then decided to investigate the situation of the refugee camps in the American occupation zones in Europe. He appointed Earl Harrison, Dean of the Pennsylvania University Law School and Former Commissioner of Immigration, to investigate the D.P. refugee situation in the American zones. He also turned to Dr. Joseph Schwartz, Director of the Joint Distribution Committee in Europe to assist Harrison. In July of 1945, Harrison set out for Europe and submitted his first impressions at the end of July 1945. The final report was submitted on August 24 1945 to the president. The findings were pretty bad. Harrison accused the USA army of inhuman conduct towards Jewish D.P.s. They were still fenced in by barbed wire and guarded by soldiers.

Many of them were still wearing the rags from the camps. The report also suggested that 100,000 Jewish D.P.s should be permitted to go to Palestine. Most of the Jewish D.P.s wanted to go to their own place like other nationals. The president read the report and ordered the military to take steps to implement the recommendations of the Harrison report. General Eisenhower, Supreme Allied Commander, issued specific orders to the military establishment in the American zones to implement the recommendations, notably the establishment of Jewish D.P. camps, removal of barbed wires, soldiers, and the establishment of elective representation in the camps. Most military commanders implemented the recommendation. President Truman seriously considered the Harrison proposal to send some of the Jewish D.P.s to Palestine and to the USA. The British refused to listen and insisted on continuing their policy of no Jewish emigration to Palestine.

Earl Harrison, Dean of the Pennsylvania University Law School

The American army implemented the Harrison recommendations in the refugee camps under their control but some officers resented the policy and General George Patton, Commander of the third American Army decided to take steps to stop the flow of Jewish refugees to his sector that extended into Czechoslovakia near Pilsen. The Karlov camp, an UNRRA refugee camp, was established in this zone. The "Brichah" began using Karlov as a staging point to smuggle Jewish refugees in transit in Czechoslovakia across this American enclave to the American zone in Germany.

In the spring of 1945, three transports totalling about 600 Jewish refugees arrived from Czechoslovakia and entered the Karlov camp. The refugees were accepted and registered by the camp officials. But Patton ordered his men to round up the 600 refugees, put them back on a train, and send them out of the American zone back into Czechoslovakia, (see New York Post Oct 2, 1945 and New York Post October 7, 1945). The screaming headlines of the New York Post told the story. The description of how Jewish Holocaust survivors were being dragged by American soldiers to the trucks was fully described. President Truman was furious. He had already signed the "Harrison Report" in 1945 that called for the decent treatment of Jewish survivors in the D.P. Camps in Germany and Austria.

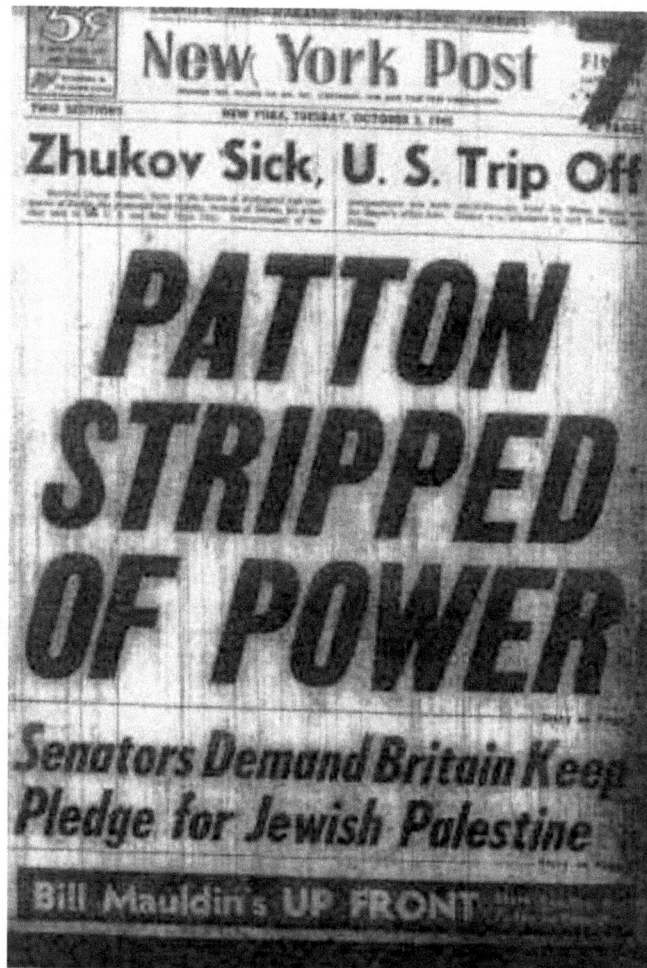

New York Post front page dated October 2 1945

Truman and Eisenhower were deeply embarrassed by the American Army's actions.

Here is a typical report of the event:

"Patton Turned Back 600 Jews Fleeing Terror in Poland"
by Pat Frank

Pilsen, Czechoslovakia, Oct. 2. At the order of Gen. Patton, 600 Polish Jews who hoped they had reached asylum in the U.S. zone from an anti–Semitic wave of terror sweeping their homeland, were forcibly returned to that country, this correspondent established today.

A Munich cable on Sept 21 reported that 650 Jews who had escaped from Poland had arrived via Prague at the Pilsen reception camp a month before. Interrogated by American officers, they sought to pass themselves off as German Jews desiring to return to Munich. Their faulty German, however, gave them away, after which "an American general," the cable stated, ordered them all returned to Poland. The anti–Semitic terror in Poland was attested to by Jews who have escaped to the American zone.

Ike's Policy Ignored

At least 3,000 Polish Jews have reached the U.S. zone. What happened to the 600 who believed they had found refuge at Camp Karlov, the United Nations' displaced persons center here, is another story. The tale is nearly as shocking as what happened to them when they were returned from Nazi concentration camps to their homes in Poland. Gen. Patton's 22nd Corps, stationed in the U.S. zone in Czechoslovakia, violated the oft–repeated policy of Gen. Eisenhower – that refugees or persecuted peoples who do not desire to return to their homelands, or whose lives would be endangered in so doing, would not be returned by force. Furthermore, it is to be noted that Jews alone were singled out for forcible return. The Jews began crowding into Camp Karlov around the middle of August. Three trains, each carrying 175, arrived at the Pilsen railway station, temporary American zone in Czechoslovakia. Others, on foot, sought refuge here after trudging through the Russian zone in Czechoslovakia. The top authorities of the 22nd Corps requested permission to ship these Jews to Germany where special camps for Jews were being erected. But Gen. Patton's headquarters ordered them shipped back to Czechoslovakia. It is somewhat complicated to trace the exact responsibility for this order since the D.P. officers then in charge of Camp Karlov have been redeployed. However the officers now in charge say that Gen. Patton's 3rd Army headquarters ordered the Jews returned because "there wasn't room for any more Jews in Germany, where the camps are already overcrowded" and "the trains that brought those Jews entered our zone without proper authority." To this correspondent, enlisted men at Camp Karlov described the pitiful scenes that ensued when the 600 Jews were loaded aboard trucks, on Aug. 24, and taken to the Pilsen railroad station. The women among them fought bitterly, screaming and kicking.

We Had To Use Force

The military detachment found itself unable to cope with the situation and asked for assistance. The 8th Armored Division sent troops with rifles, machine–guns and armored vehicles. Pvt. Edward Heilbrun, of Chicago, who is Jewish and who helped to load the hapless, protesting Jews aboard the trucks, told me: "My job was sickening. Men threw themselves on their knees in front of me, tore open their shirts, and screamed, 'Kill me now!' They would say, 'You might just as well kill me now. I am dead anyway if I go back to Poland.' "They kept jumping off the trucks. And we had to use force." There was more trouble at the railroad station where the troops were forced to jam the 600 Jews aboard a train."

Destination a Mystery

After the train started, the trouble continued, according to witnesses. Men threw themselves from the moving train. Troops fired in the air attempting to frighten them into remaining on the train. Where the train was routed, after leaving the American zone, is still a mystery. One woman who was scheduled to return to Poland did not have to go. Luba Zindel of Cracow, was having a baby at the hospital when the train departed. I talked to her at Camp Karlov. This is her story: With her husband and an earlier child, she had spent three years in the Nazi concentration camp at Lublin. After the Russians captured that city, the family was released. They returned to their home in Cracow on June 20 1945. On the first Saturday in August, while the family was attending services, the synagogue was attacked and stormed by uniformed AK troopers. "They were shouting, she told me that we had committed ritual murders. They began firing at us and beating us. My husband was sitting beside me. He fell down on his face, full of bullets."

"The widow was among those selected by the Jewish Committee in Cracow to be given a chance to escape to Czechoslovakia. She arrived here aboard the first of three trains".

The train with the Jewish refugees was forced to leave the American enclave and crossed the Czech border. The train was stopped and the passengers were removed by the Czech Brichah to temporary shelters where they were fed and rested. All the refugees would cross the border again but in smaller groups led by the Brichah. General Patton was of course dismissed from his post, and no further attempt would be made by the American army to stop Jewish refugees entering the American zones. Toman was very pleased with the results since he could continue to permit Jewish refugees to cross Czechoslovakia.

All these American activities surrounding Jewish refugees drove Britain mad. They looked for ways to reduce the preoccupation with the Jewish refugees. They wanted America to act like Britain, notably ignore the Jewish problem in Europe. Britain claimed that it did not check the religion of the refugees. Yes, there were refugees in the British zones of Germany and Austria but these were former nationals of European countries. "But we do not have Jewish refugees; we have Polish, Hungarian and Slovakian refugees. We deal with these refugees." The British refused to acknowledge that some of the Poles and Hungarians were Jews. And, since they were not Jews, just Poles or Hungarians, there was no Jewish problem. On instruction from London, the British military authorities in their zones of occupation refused to recognize the elected representative of the Jewish D.P.s in the Bergen–Belsen camp, Josef Rosensaft. He was elected on April 17, 1945, two days after the camp was liberated. Bergen–Belsen was the largest Jewish D.P. camp in the British zone in Germany. It contained about 10,346 Jewish refugees. The entire Jewish D.P. population in the British zone in Germany was 12,232 and this number hardly changed. Even British Jewish social services were not permitted to enter D.P. camps in the British zones. The British government was determined to hide the Jewish problem in Europe by any and all means. But Jewish refugees kept entering Germany and Austria and then headed to the Mediterranean ports where they boarded illegal ships that set out for Palestine. The illegal fleet of the Brichah increased with the arrival of American ships and American crews notably the "*Exodus*" ship. These ships received wide coverage in the American press and created a climate of anti–British feeling. The British tried to stop the campaign by seizing the illegal ships on the high seas and sent the passengers to the Cyprus detention camps. More ships continued to arrive and ever more screaming pictures and headlines of British soldiers mishandling Jewish Holocaust survivors appeared in the press.

Lieutenant–General Sir Frederick Morgan

Britain was desperate and tried to combat this opinion. British officials everywhere were urged to present these Jewish refugees as wild terrorists. British officials of course followed British foreign policy directives and repeated the wild stories about the Soviet agents wearing Zionist clothing. The most publicized event was of course the press conference held by the UNRRA Director of European Operations, Lieutenant-General Sir Frederick Morgan, on January 3 1946 in Frankfurt, Germany. The general stated that "he was not impressed by all the talk about pogroms within Poland". Furthermore he stated that "a Jewish secret force is organizing the exodus of Jews from Europe and added that Jews fleeing from Poland to Berlin were well-dressed, well-fed, rosy-cheeked and have plenty of money". There were elements of truth in these words namely the Brichah operations of smuggling Jews out of Eastern Europe but the crude anti-Semitic presentations created a storm in the Jewish world, especially in the USA which was the main financial backer of the UNRRA. Of course, the general, who was ostensibly in charge of helping poor and destitute refugees, Jewish and non-Jewish, attempted to soften the impact of his crude statements by claiming he was misunderstood or misquoted or both. He was certainly understood as representing British foreign policy. But the American press was against Morgan and insisted on action. Fiorello La Guardia, head of UNRRA had no choice but to dismiss Morgan from his post. Morgan protested the dismissal. Bevin strongly backed Morgan. The USA did not want to create a greater gap than already existed between the two countries. La Guardia had to reinstate Morgan. Morgan continued to make embarrassing anti-Semitic statements to the detriment of UNRRA and himself.

American Jewish organizations were furious with Morgan's anti-Semitic statements and demanded to dismiss him permanently from office. In London, British Jewry was also pressuring for his dismissal as well as an opening of access to the Jewish Holocaust survivors in the British zone of occupation. American pressure forced the British authorities to ease up on the strict policies that they enforced against the Jewish refugees.

The British government ultimately dismissed Morgan from his post after criticizing incompetence and corruption within UNRRA. The general claimed that UNRRA was diverting resources to Zionist causes.

President Truman decided to appoint Simon H. Rifkind, a US District Court Judge for the southern district of New York, as a civilian Special Advisor on Jewish Affairs in Europe. Judge Rifkind was sent to Europe in November 1945 to tour UNRRA facilities and prepare a report. Judge Rifkind was highly respected both by the army and the various charitable organizations.

GENERAL MORGAN REINSTATED

Post With UNRRA

LONDON, Jan. 30 (A.A.P.). The UNRRA office in Great Britain has announced that Lieutenant-General Sir Frederick Morgan has succeeded in his appeal against termination of his appointment as chief of UNRRA operations in Germany.

[Early in January General Morgan said at a Press conference that a secret Jewish organisation was promoting the exodus of thousands of Jews from Poland to the United States zone in Germany. After protests by Jewish organisations, UNRRA headquarters asked for his resignation. An investigation by the United States Third Army resulted in a report supporting General Morgan's statement.]

When he first arrived Rifkind served under Allied Commander for the European Theater General Dwight D.Eisenhower, but "Ike" left his post a month after Rifkind arrived. Rifkind then served Eisenhower's replacement, General Joseph T. McNarney. The judge stayed in Europe until March 1946.

Years later Judge Rifkind's son Robert said that the six months his father had spent in Europe had made him much more of a cynic, having witnessed first–hand the devilry that the Germans had committed, and the unjust discrimination these same Jews, who managed to survive, were still suffering. According to Robert Rifkind, his father said that almost all the Jewish refugees he encountered wanted to go to Palestine. Nowhere else.

Not long after Rifkind arrived in Europe, David Ben Gurion, Chairman of the Jewish Agency Executive arrived from Jerusalem to visit the "saved remnants" of the Jewish people. He was greeted with great enthusiasm.

Judge Simon Rifkind (on left)

Rabbi Samuel Abramovitz, then a young man recently released from the US Army, was volunteering with the JDC in a German D.P. camp. According to Abramovitz, who went on to a long distinguished career with the JDC, Ben Gurion was "greeted like a king." Crowds turned out waving flags and cheering.

The British ambassador to Prague, Philip Nichols, demanded that Czechoslovakia close the borders the day following the Kielce pogrom in Poland. He even insisted that Jacobson be expelled from Czechoslovakia[7]. The American ambassador to Prague, Lawrence Steinhardt, consistently pressured Czechoslovakia to close the borders to Polish Jewish refugees. The Czechs replied that only refugees with legal papers were permitted to travel through Czechoslovakia. Still the ambassador protested; he was urged to complain in writing which he did. The letter was received by Masaryk. He leaked a copy of the letter to Toman. Toman invited Steinhardt to his office and told him: "I (Toman) am going to send the National Guard and they will take you out of the office, and like a sack of potatoes we shall throw you out.[8]" Toman was furious that Steinhardt, a Jew, fought so hard against his own people in trouble. Furthermore, Steinhardt supposedly suggested that Toman be removed from his office since he was Jewish. This incensed Toman. The contents of the protest letter were published in Paris and created a sensation that embarrassed the president of the USA[9].Even the Russian ambassador to Prague, Valery Zorin, notified Gottwald that Czechoslovakia permitted too many Polish Jews to cross the country. Gottwald called on Toman and showed him the letter. Toman managed to get himself off the hook by stating that he was fighting the Anglo–American imperialistic plots aimed against the Communist world[10]. Still the trains with illegal Jews continued to roll.

Lawrence Steinhardt, USA ambassador to Prague

Britain saw the widening rift between the USA and herself regarding Jewish immigration to Palestine. Bevin decided to heal the rift by proposing the creation of a combined committee to study the entire problem and make binding recommendations. Truman accepted the proposal. The governments of Britain and the United States formed the Anglo–American Commission for Palestine to devise a policy that could be recommended regarding the immigration of Jews to Palestine. Other committees also examined the situation in Palestine, but this was the only committee that also included the conditions of the Jews left in Europe as part of their considerations. The committee would consist of six Americans and six British members. The findings would be binding. Britain packed its delegation with supporters of British foreign policy and was certain that it would get some American votes in the committee; thus the British position would always be supported or at worst, there would be a tie within the committee. Not only did the committee visit the United States and London, Arab capitals and Palestine, but also D.P. camps in Europe. There they questioned Jewish Holocaust survivors. Most of the survivors said they wanted to move to Palestine. Professor Chaim Weitzman, head of the World Zionist Organization and David Ben Gurion, head of the Jewish Agency in Palestine addressed the commission. Rabbi Herzog testified before the commission on behalf of a Jewish state, claiming that the new Jewish entity could absorb all the Jewish survivors in Europe. He also testified to what he had personally witnessed in the Italian D.P. camps. Rabbi Herzog was well prepared and eloquently presented his case with biblical quotations and references to Jewish history, namely Jews pray three times a day to Zion.

Ben Gurion (back row) beside Rabbi Herzog, at Commission meeting on Mt. Scopus, Jerusalem

The commission's final report, issued in October 1946, recommended Jewish immigration of 100,000 refugees to Palestine. Britain rejected the findings, in spite of its commitments to the contrary. Bevin shamelessly dropped the report that he himself proposed, in the waste basket. Truman was angry and felt a bit betrayed by his British ally. Britain continued to adhere to its policy as though nothing had happened. Britain continued to issue only 1,500 entry certificates a month until the number reached the original *White Paper's* 75,000, mostly those interred in the Cyprus refugee camps, built to house immigrants caught trying to illegally enter Palestine.'

The American ambassador to Prague was usually well disposed to Jews and their problems but the State Department's pressure was relentless.

1946. Polish–Czech border

Palestinian emissary of the Brichah Bobo Landau, Czech border guard official, Joint Director in Prague Gaynor Jacobson, Inspector Dohacz and the commander of the border post. Jacobson checked the crossing facilities for Jewish refugees that kept coming to Czechoslovakia

He protested time and again against the open door policy of the Czech government. The American ambassador consistently pressured Czechoslovakia to close the borders to Polish Jewish refugees.

The Czechs, or rather Toman ignored these protests by claiming ignorance of border crossings. The American and British ambassadors were desperate but could do little since the Czech officials kept the borders open. Even Russia became perturbed by the mass exit of Jews and the Russian ambassador to Prague, Valery Zorin, wrote a letter to Gottwald demanding explanations. Gottwald called Toman and asked for explanations. Toman provided some answers, notably that the Anglo–American imperialists wanted the Czechs to be their policeman. Refugees cross the border legally in accordance with UNRRA agreements. Gottwald told Zorin what Toman said. Zorin was not terribly pleased with the answers but decided not to make an issue since he was busy planning to seize power in Czechoslovakia and wanted the Czech Communist party to be united and ready for action The Jewish refugee transports kept rolling and the D.P. camps were constantly expanding.

1946. Jewish refugees leaving Czechoslovakia

Footnotes

1. Moshe Arens, *Flags over the Ghetto of Warsaw*, Gefen Publishing Company, USA, p.80
2. Szulc, Alliance p29
3. Zertel, Power. p.20
4. San Francisco Jewish Community Publications Inc. *JWeekly.com*"*Deaths of 260 in 1940 ship explosion commemorated*". 14 December 2001. Retrieved 25 May 2013.
5. Kochavi, Post'p.40
6. Kochavi, Post'p.40
7. Szulc, Alliance, p.155
8. Szulc, Alliance, p.157
9. Szulc, Alliance, p.157
10. Szulc, Alliance, p.155

Chapter VII
The Mass Exit Continues

Jewish refugees arriving at Nachod

Transports of Jewish refugees kept arriving at the Czech borders and Germany in spite of all the British and American protests to the Czech government. As long as the government did not order the borders totally closed, Toman kept them open. Most transports remained a few days on Czech soil and continued their journey to Germany or Austria and hence to Italy or France for the refugees to board illegal ships and head to Palestine. The British government was determined to break this pattern. It decided to attack the Czech government through internal pressures. Items began to appear in the Czech press claiming that the government was spending money it did not have on refugees crossing the country. The campaign picked up speed as the days went by.

Far left: Gaynor Jacobson on Polish/Czech border

According to Jacobson, the Czechs had established an efficient machinery to handle the flow of Jewish refugees. The Czech government established a committee comprised of the Welfare and Labor Ministry, the Foreign Affairs Ministry and the Interior Ministry. This committee worked in conjunction with the Czech JDC office and local Czech Jewish community representatives. Together they handled all the problems that arose, keeping the Jewish refugees flowing smoothly through Czechoslovakia[1].

Crises were as constant as the sun and the moon. The number of refugees was increasing rapidly and so were the expenses. According to Jacobson, from January 5th 1946 to the beginning of July 1946 the Czech government spent 21 million Czech korunas (crowns) ($420,000) on food alone.[2] And the Jewish exodus from Eastern Europe had just begun. Then the Czech trains began to roll. Trains were the only way to efficiently and quickly deal with the mass of people crossing the country.

According to William Leibner who crossed the border illegally, the trek went something like this: Jews arrived at the Polish border in small groups, many by truck, and some on Polish trains that stopped at the last railway station on the Polish side. The refugees went to a pre–arranged meeting point where the Brichah guides were waiting to take them across the borders in small groups. Most of the Jewish refugees crossed the border on foot while a few managed to cross aboard trucks.

Once the refugees reached the Czechoslovakian side, the small groups gathered at one of a few staging areas, either at the large camps the Czech government set up at Nachod or Broumow, or other smaller camps. The small Jewish refugee groups were then combined into larger groups and put on trains bound for Austria and Germany. Rarely did the groups spend more than a day at the camps, although sometimes two or three days were needed to organize the transports.

Once the Czech trains reached the Austrian or German border, the refugees disembarked, the Brichah again divided the refugees up into smaller groups that surreptitiously found their way across the Austrian or German borders. The Brichah then transported the refugees on trucks borrowed from UNRRA, the JDC, or the American Army.[3] The Czechs had been assured that UNRRA would assume most of the costs of transportation, temporary lodging and food for the transient Jewish refugees. In preliminary discussions with the local UNRRA chief in Czechoslovakia, Mr. Elfam Rhees, regarding these expenses, Rhees intimated that UNRRA would assume the costs, or a good portion of them.

But there was obvious discrimination. The Czechs were shocked when they learned that UNRRA refused to pay bills concerning transport of these Jewish refugees.

The UNRRA office readily paid transportation bills and other expenses for the transport of non–Jews while payment for the transport of Jews dragged on. UNRRA officials easily determined which was which. Almost all the passengers on transports originating at the Polish borders heading toward Austria or Germany were Jewish refugees. The non–payment of the bills increased the expenses of the Czech government. The British and American campaign indirectly exploited this state of affairs through their press connections.

The Czech Deputy Interior Minister, Zdenek Toman, who was in charge of the borders, insisted that the transports of illegal Jews continue even as more bills were presented to UNRRA. But as trains of Jewish refugees rolled across Czechoslovakia, the costs continued to climb, with no reimbursements forthcoming. The fact UNRRA received the bills did not mean all the bills were paid. UNRRA decided which bills to pay and the Czech government frequently received less than they spent.

Toman later said, in an interview to Tad Szulc, "Had a non–Jew occupied my post, he would have definitely stopped the trains and other expenses until payment was made[4].

"The fact that transportation costs and other expenses soared did not seem to bother Toman. As he said, as long as he was in power, Czechoslovakia would continue to physically provide transportation for the Jewish refugees.[5]

Some Czech newspapers began to discuss the fact that UNRRA was not paying for the refugees and the expenses were being shouldered by the Czech government that could ill afford them. The topic was even discussed on the radio. These discussions received a tremendous boost when Mary Gibbons, Deputy Assistant Director of UNRRA Operations for Europe arrived in Prague. On July 7, 1946, three days after the Kielce pogrom that left 42 Jewish survivors dead, she publicly stated that UNRRA would not pay for Jewish Polish refugees who crossed Czechoslovakia since they had already been repatriated to their homes following the war.[6] She continued to repeat this statement throughout Czechoslovakia until July 14, 1946 when she left the country.

According to the JDC's Gaynor Jacobson, Mrs. Gibbons repeated the same statements over and over, from July 7 to July 14, 1946, in every meeting she had with Czech ministers, high officials and the press.[7]

The publicized statements by Mary Gibbons of UNRRA had one objective, notably to force Czechoslovakia to close the borders and not permit Jewish refugees to transit the countries. Britain had to stop the illegal ships with Jewish refugees that were embarrassing England throughout the world, especially in the USA. The pictures showing British soldiers manhandling Holocaust survivors undermined world public opinion in Britain's ability to control and rule Palestine.

Gibbons was not concerned with UNRRA but rather with British foreign policy. We already mentioned General Morgan's statements pertaining to Jewish Holocaust survivors. The statements created a storm of protests in the USA. Jewish organizations were outraged by these veiled anti-Semitic statements dressed up in humanitarian clothing. Congressmen and senators received mail expressing indignation at these statements. UNRRA offices began to explain that the statements were reported incorrectly or they were misquoted out of context. The Czech press and many government officials only saw that Czechoslovakia would have to pay large amounts of money which it did not have. Czech cabinet ministers began to discuss the situation.

UNRRA had not paid for the repatriation of the Polish citizens who had been in Russia during the war. Their repatriation was covered by the Russian–Polish repatriation agreements. The fact that the Jews decided to leave their so-called new homes out of self-protection did not faze Gibbons. Gibbon's political motives were clear. Britain wanted Czechoslovakian borders closed so that Jewish refugees could not sail to Palestine. Still, the mass exodus of European Jews was in full swing, and the Czechs continued the transient program, the bills increased daily, and the expenses mounted like stacks of hay during a harvest.

The Czech press and radio carried the news of Gibbons' statement. Hearing that the Czech government was not to be reimbursed, many Czech officials panicked. The situation was exacerbated by the British and American embassies in Prague. There, embassy officials did their best to incite fear in the public's mind: the idea that the Czechs would be stuck paying all the bills for the Jewish refugees, bills the government could ill-afford.

The theme espoused by the British and American embassies and Gibbons was seized upon by the local press. The country was just starting to find some traction after years of Nazi occupation. The Czech economy was struggling, the government nearly bankrupt, and unemployment was high. Clearly, the Czech people were opposed to the use of the little money they had going to help Jewish refugees. Most believed the country could ill afford these expenses.

The fears, rumors and harsh criticisms soon reached the ears of government ministers. The government met on July 16, 1946, and a heated discussion ensued regarding the Polish Jewish refugees crossing Czechoslovakia[8]. Many ministers favored halting the program, but Foreign Minister Jan Masaryk threatened to resign if the cabinet stopped the Jewish refugee transit program.[9] The cabinet was seriously divided on the issue. But Masaryk's intervention put a stop to the cabinet discussion. The issue was rescheduled for further discussion.

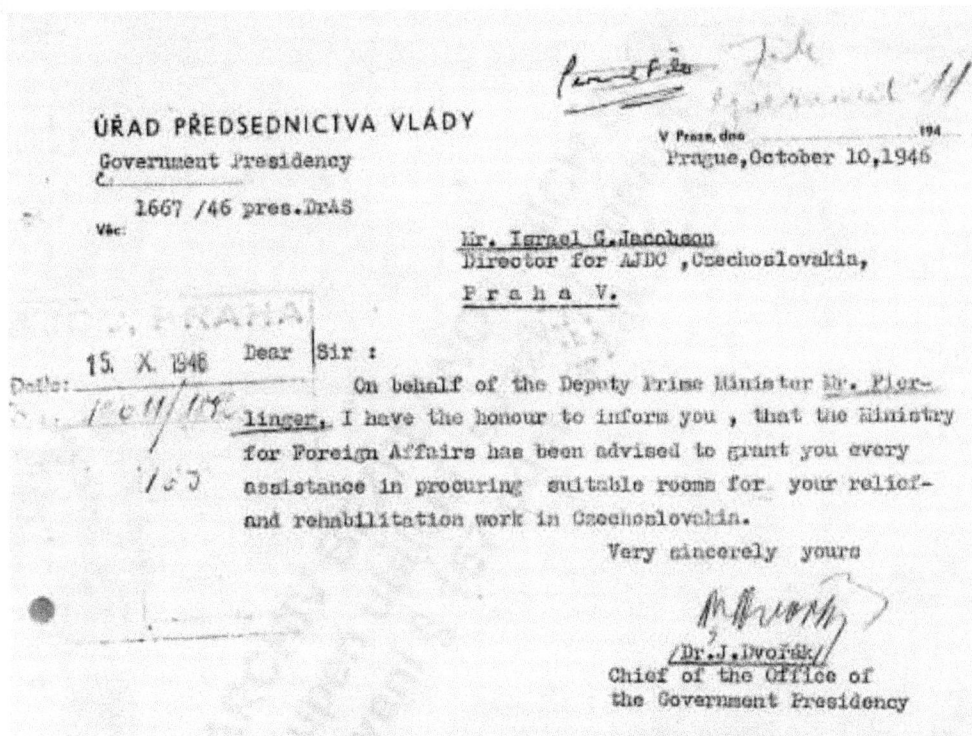

Czech government offering help to the Joint in Prague

Meanwhile, the borders stayed open and the flow of refugees increased hourly. To facilitate the flow of Polish Jewish refugees, the JDC received permission to extend the reception facilities at the transit camps. The European Joint organization sent massive supplies of food, clothing and medical supplies to the border camps to provide the Polish Jewish transients with their basic needs. The Czech government placed many facilities at the disposal of the Joint organization, and permitted the expansion of existing facilities namely Nahod, which could handle up to 1,000 people.

The Joint and the Brichah worked hand in hand to move this mass of people across Czechoslovakia. The operation threatened to collapse on a few occasions but it continued to roll until most of the Jews that wanted to, had left Eastern Europe.

The Joint offices in Czechoslovakia and Poland were placed on a military footing to cope with the impending mass movements. The Brichah mobilized all its forces to deal with the transports. Jews crossed the Polish–Czech borders prior to this agreement but the numbers were relatively small. In May of 1946 3,052 Polish Jews crossed illegally to Czechoslovakia, in June 8,000, in July 19,000, in August 35,346, and in September 1946, 12,379 Jews crossed the border illegally[10]. During five months 77,777 Polish Jews crossed the Czech–Polish border at a single place called Nachod. The camp was set up on the Czech side. Of course, there were other crossing points in Czechoslovakia namely Brumov, where another temporary refugee camp was established. Both camps provided the refugees with a resting place, some food and medical attention if needed prior to moving to the next place. There were a few other smaller camps along the Czech border.

Letter sent by Jacobson to the Joint Office in New York requesting that the office publicize the activities of Czechoslovakia on behalf of the Jewish refugees

The Polish and Czech border guards cooperated with each other and with the Brichah officials of Poland and Czechoslovakia. Transports were handled quickly and efficiently unless there was a backup along the American–German or American–Austrian frontiers when the borders were shut as it happened on several occasions[11]. Here is a description of a JTA correspondent at the scene;

'All night long. Every night little groups of Jewish refugees stream across the Polish border into the little town known as Nachod in Czechoslovakia. Sometimes their clothes are wet up to their waist, their eyes are red and bloated from the strain of trying to see through the darkness. Their backs are bent.' The same author writes: *'The Czech–Polish border was reopened last night after being closed for three days. Additional trains have been placed on the Nachod–Bratislava run to speed movements of the Jewish refugees. Earlier, the Prague radio had said that the frontier had been closed following British intervention. But the frontiers were always reopened following heavy pressures on the involved parties be it in Washington or Prague. Some Polish Jews were shipped by rail to Bratislava and then Austria, while others were sent directly to the American zone of Germany.'*

Zdenek Toman was familiar with most of the Joint and Brichah activities in Czechoslovakia since he had agents everywhere that reported to him. He of course knew that the Brichah had a transmitter, since his office permitted the item to be brought from Belgium and installed in Prague. He was even aware of the bribes that were paid along the road and borders by the Brichah officials as they travelled to and from Czechoslovakia. His office kept an eye on all these activities. Toman, Jacobson and Goberman worked together to solve the various problems that occurred along the road. Toman constantly urged Jacobson to publish the activities of the Czech government on behalf of the Polish Jewish refugees in the American press to create a cordial atmosphere for Czechoslovakia in the US. The Joint established or supported orphanages and rest homes for the needy Czech Jewish survivors as well as medical centers. All of these activities made a good impression on the Czech government and the Czech population at large. The Joint organization was held in high esteem for the valuable social work it did in Czechoslovakia following the war. See the complimentary letters sent by government officials to Jacobson.

TRANSLATION

PRIME MINISTER
No. 988

Prague, March 24th, 1947

Mr. Director:

I received your news about a check amounting to $1,000.
for children in communities affected by the recent floods.

I thank you very much for your gift. I am convinced
that it will be a welcome contribution to the mitigation of
great distress caused by the floods.

Please receive the expression of my sincere esteem

Gottwald

Mr. Israel G. Jacobson
Director AJDC Czechoslovakia
Praha V
Josefovska 7

Czech prime minister thanks Jacobson for the help extended to the flood victims

But the issue of the transit program for Polish Jewish refugees stayed hot. The Czech cabinet continued their discussions; more meetings were held between various ministers, party officials, even with Czech social service organizations, UNRRA and JDC officials. Meetings were held in the cabinet, conferences were held between the involved Ministers of Interior, Welfare, and Foreign Affairs, and Joint and UNRRA officials. Toman of course kept Jacobson informed of the dealings behind the scenes. At a dinner meeting, Toman informed Jacobson that unless the Joint took drastic action, the Czech government would be forced to close the borders.[12] The implication was clear that even he, Toman, would have to bow to the will of the cabinet and close the borders. Toman further pointed out to Jacobson that the Soviets were taking an interest in the transit of Jews in Czechoslovakia. We already mentioned the letter of Zorin to Gottwald. Now, Peter I. Alexeev, head of UNRRA's Russian mission in Prague, actually chief resident of the Soviet NKVD in Czechoslovakia was dead set against helping Polish Jewish refugees cross into and through Czechoslovakia.[13]

While the Soviet Union granted more flexibility to the Czech government than to any other country under its hegemony, Alexeev and his staff in Prague did everything in their power to undermine the Czech government's stand on Jewish refugees. Alexeev, under orders from Moscow, did his best to sabotage UNRRA's efforts helping Jewish refugees in Czechoslovakia.[14]

Moscow knew when and how to apply pressure. Alexeev told his bosses, and the Czechs, "There are small numbers of Polish refugees in Czechoslovakia and the government can handle the problem."[15] The implication was clear: the present number of Polish refugees could be handled but if the number of refugees continued to increase, the Czechs would have problems with the Soviets.

These Soviet hints altered the mood of the Czech cabinet. The cabinet was heading towards closing the transit program according to Toman unless the Joint organization acted[16]. Toman advised Jacobson to take whatever drastic action he could to influence the cabinet to keep the borders open. Both Toman and Jacobson knew that if the borders were closed the Jewish Holocaust survivors would be stuck in Eastern Europe and would be at the mercy of the rising anti–Semitism. Worse, Jacobson knew that if the borders were closed the flood of refugees making their way to Palestine would stop cold.

Jacobson immediately contacted the JDC's European head Joseph Schwartz who was at the time in Hungary. They set up a meeting in Vienna.[17] Also invited to the meeting was Pinkas Lubianer (later Pinhas Lavon) then the Jewish Agency representative in Prague, later important politician in Israel. In Vienna the three men discussed the situation. Jacobson and Lubianer traveled to Austria together by train. While on a flight from Hungary to France, Jacobson met Schwartz[18] in Vienna, and informed him of the latest developments, and urged decisions[19]. Schwartz immediately granted an automatic grant of $20,000 dollars or 1.000.000 Czech korunas to help pay for the Polish Jewish refugee program[20]. The news was relayed to the Czech cabinet and then released to the press at large. Schwartz also cabled appeals to the board of governors of the Joint in New York and explained the desperate situation. He urged immediate action before the Czechs closed the borders. The Joint headquarters in New York began to pressure the US government and the UNRRA general offices in New York regarding the statements made by Miss Gibbons. In Prague, Deputy Interior Minister Zdenek Toman was keeping the JDC's Gaynor Jacobson fully informed of the behind–the–scenes dealings of the Czech government to allow the transports to continue. But Toman informed Jacobson of a new and very serious complication.

The JDC headquarters in New York responded by publishing the statements made by Miss Gibbons in order to put pressure on whomever they could, from New York Governor Herbert Lehman, to the newly appointed director of the UNRRA Fiorello LaGuardia, former mayor of New York City, all the way up to the U.S. government.

THREESIXTEEN YOUR FIVEFORTY LAGUARDIA LEFT YESTERDAY DUE CAIRO JULI
FIFTEEN ATHENS EIGHTEENTH ROME TWENTYFIRST BELGRADE TWENTYFIFTH PARIS
THIRTIETH GENEVE AUGUST FOURTH FOR UNRRA COUNCIL MEETING STOP
DISCUSSED CONTENTS YOUR CABLE WITH UNRRA WASHINGTON WHO ADVISED UNDER-
STANDING WITH CZECHOSLOVAKIA PROVIDES THAT CZECHOSLOVAKIA WILL GIVE
NECESSARY ASSISTANCE TO POSTWAR REFUGEES COMING UNDER UNRRA CARE SUCH
AS PRESENT INFILTREES STOP CZECHOSLOVAKIA HAS RIGHT REQUEST ADDITION-
AL SUPPLIES BASIS THESE EXTRAORDINARY EXPENDITURES WITH RESUMPTION
CZECHOSLOVAKIAN UNRRA MUST BE WITHIN CZECHOSLOVAKIAN BORDER BUT RE-
QUESTS FOR ADDITIONAL ASSISTANCE WILL BE CONSIDERED STOP UNRRA
CABLING LONDON THAT NO CHANGE THIS UNDERSTANDING SO FAR AS KNOWN
HERE NO REQUEST HAS BEEN RECEIVED CZECHOSLOVAKIA FOR ADDITIONAL ALLOT-
MENT STOP PLEASE KEEP US ADVISED IN ORDER TO FOLLOW UP WITH UNRRA
WASHINGTON.

Cable dated July 19, 1946, sent from New York to Schwartz in Paris and a copy to Jacobson in Prague

The pressure of the Jewish organizations in America had their effect. Soon the following cable reply dated July 19, 1946 arrived in Prague. There was no change of UNRRA policy, the Polish Jewish refugees were entitled to all the help that UNRRA provided. If further needs were required, the Czech government could request them. The cable further stated that the UNRRA office in Washington wanted explanations from the UNRRA office in London regarding the so–called change of policy[21]. The cable in essence revealed that London was playing games without consulting Washington, the main contributor of the UNRRA program. The cable was presented to Toman who forwarded it to the cabinet. Obviously Britain decided to force Czechoslovakia into action and staged the panic. The actions of the Joint somewhat defused the crisis. The official announcement that the Joint would provide additional sums of money to Czechoslovakia further calmed the situation in Prague.

Toman continued to meet Jacobson and they discussed plans of speeding up the passage of the Jewish refugees through Czechoslovakia. Plans were also established to enlarge the reception facilities for the ever increasing number of refugees. Toman also expressed fear that there might be Ukrainian fascists and other undesirables crossing the Czech borders mixed with the Jewish refugees. Jacobson assured him that the Brichah agents would prevent non–Jews from entering the Jewish transport groups. The possibility of asking Poland to regulate the flow of Jewish refugees was also considered but the idea was dropped. Each country acted in secret and once you start regulations you never know where they end. Toman even promised to return to the Joint a fine of 115.000 ($2300) Czech korunas that was imposed on Jews that crossed the Czech border illegally[22]. The Joint paid the fine and the Jewish refugees continued their journey. Toman further stated that he had helped and would continue to help the Jewish refugees to cross Czechoslovakia to reach Germany and Austria. In the interview for the Brichah movie[23], Toman openly stated that he could have closed or opened the borders without consulting other officials. According to him (Toman), he decided when the borders would be open and who would cross them. In this spirit he sent an order to all the border guard posts not to stop Jewish refugees that entered Czechoslovakia even if they did not have the necessary legal papers[24].

Train with Jewish refugees heading west in Czechoslovakia

The Czech Brichah office in Prague headed by Moshe Goberman took the Jewish refugees to the various borders and out of the country. Each train carried about 1,000 Jews. The trains usually stopped at Brno at night where the transients were fed hot meals served by the local Jewish community. The food of course was provided by the Czech Joint[25]. Practically no convoys of Jews were directed through the city of Prague unless it was unavoidable for fear of alarming Czech officials or media. Toman kept the trains moving and ordered all Czech border guards to let Jews pass the borders with or without papers, and Jacobson and Moshe Govsman (head of the Mossad in Czechoslovakia) kept the convoys of Jews moving across the Czech borders. Thousands of Czechoslovak, Hungarian, Ukrainian, Romanian and Baltic Jews joined the Polish exodus. The UNRRA finally paid the Czech government $225,000 late in the fall of 1946[26] to cover the old debt that by now reached a million dollars. The Joint also decided to contribute some money to the debt but it was never completely repaid[27].

Problems occurred with some transports and Toman, Jacobson and the Brichah had their hands full. They worked hand in hand to keep the operation moving in spite of all the obstacles and problems along the way.

The UNRRA assurances that the bills would be paid and the publicized Joint grants to the Czech government had their desired effect. The Czech cabinet voted to continue the refugee program and to keep the borders open[28]. The cabinet also decided to limit the stay of the transient Jewish Polish refugees to a minimum number of days on Czech soil, to pressure the UNRRA to settle the refugee bills and to increase the allotments for the refugee transient program. Toman expressed his satisfaction with the Joint actions and continued to meet Gaynor Jacobson and even his wife Florence who also worked for the Joint in

Prague. She was a trained social worker. In the *Brichah* movie interview Florence Jacobson stated that she was terrified of Zdenek Toman. She also stated that without Toman there would not have been a mass Jewish exodus from Eastern Europe[29].

According to Tad Szulc, Toman was very proud of the fact that the borders remained open during the entire debate.[30] The UNRRA did eventually pay some of the Jewish refugees' expenses for crossing Czechoslovakia. With all the Joint and UNRRA payments, the Czech government still wound up in the red.

Philip Nichols was furious and urged Czechoslovakia to limit Jacobson's activities. The ambassador accused the Joint of bankrolling the transportation of the Jews across the country to Germany and Austria and then to Palestine.[31] There was some truth in this claim. The Joint not only provided food and medicines to the refugees but also maintained the Brichah organization financially. All Brichah officials were listed as employees of the Joint[32] and had their offices in the Joint facilities. Czechoslovakia received as many as 20 Brichah emissaries from Palestine according to Michael Hutter, a former Czech Brichah official in Czechoslovakia[33]. These officials directed the flow of refugees from the Polish borders to the German or Austrian borders. The rapid system of communications at their disposal enabled them to effectively move large masses of people across the country. Trains picked up the transients in the Nachod, Brumov and other camps and transported them to the Austrian and German borders where other guides led them to the D.P. camps.

The Czech leaders Benes, Masaryk and even to a certain extent Gottwald hoped that Russia would permit Czechoslovakia to exist like Finland. To achieve this status, Czechoslovakia needed foreign loans and financial assistance to stimulate the war dislocated economy. The only place where money was available was in New York and Masaryk mentioned at a cabinet meeting that he must meet with Baruch in New York at the next UN assembly[34]. Obviously he was going to discuss ways and means to get financial help. The Czech government wanted to create a positive picture in America. Thus the letter of Jacobson to the Joint in New York dated October 11, 1946, where he stressed the need to publicize the various Czech activities on behalf the Polish Jewish refugees that crossed Czechoslovakia[35]. The relative freedom of operation of many Jewish organizations namely the Joint, the Jewish Agency, the Brichah, the Palestinian Haganah, the Ort organization, Vaad Ha'Hatzalah and many other Jewish organizations was also part of the effort to create a positive picture in New York.

Toman of course heard about the Kielce pogrom and other acts of brutality against Jews in Poland but did not expect the refugee deluge that followed it. Toman and Jacobson kept the flood of Jewish refugees moving. The mass exodus consisted primarily of Polish Jews but there were large numbers of Latvian, Estonian, Lithuanian, Hungarian, Slovakian, Romanian, Ukrainian and some Russian Jews. The D.P. camps were bursting with Jewish refugees waiting to leave Europe. Most wanted to go to Palestine but the gates were closed.

Memorial erected for a group of "Gordonia" youth Zionists heading to the Czech border. They were attacked and killed by Poles near the city of Nowy Targ, May 1946

Footnotes

1. See Jacobson report from Prague to Paris dated 26 July 1946.
2. Ibid
3. Yehuda Bauer, *Out of the Ashes*, pp.107–108
4. Tad Szulc. *The Secret Alliance* p.158
5. Tad Szulc. *The Secret Alliance* p.158
6. Most of the Polish Jews who crossed Czechoslovakia had not been repatriated by UNRRA but by the Polish government following the war.
7. See letter of Jacobson to JDC office in New York of August 26, 1946
8. Cabinet meeting in Prague October 10, 1946.
9. Ibid
10. Yehuda Bauer, *Brichah*, p.204. Random House. New York 1970
11. See letter from Dorothy Greene
12. Tad Szulc, *The Secret Alliance*, p.159
13. Kass–interview
14. Kass–interview
15. JTA Press Release, January 4, 1946, Washington, USA
16. Tad Szulc *The Secret Alliance* p.159
17. Yehuda Bauer, *Out of the Ashes*, p.108
18. 18Yehuda Bauer, *Out of the Ashes*, p.108
19. Cable sent by Jacobson to New York
20. Cable sent by Jacobson to New York
21. Cable is in the Jacobson report of letter dated July 26th 1946.
22. Ibid. A group of Polish refugees entered Czechoslovakia illegally. They were apprehended by an overzealous guard. The case reached the court house and the judge imposed a fine of 115.000 korunas. The Joint paid the fines and the Jews continued on their journey. The Joint constantly insisted on a refund of the money. The Czech government took its time but eventually refunded the money.
23. Martin Smok– movie entitled *Brichah*.
24. Tad Szulc, *The Secret Alliance*, p.146
25. Yehuda Bauer, *Out of the Ashes*, p.109
26. Yehuda Bauer, *Brichah*, p.209. Fiorello La Guardia was soon appointed to head the UNRRA.
27. Tad Szulc, *The Secret Alliance* p.146
28. Tad Szulc *The Secret Alliance* p.159
29. Martin Smok– movie entitled *Brichah*
30. Tad Szulc, *The Secret Alliance* p.156
31. Tad Szulc, *The Secret Alliance* p.155
32. Massuah– A Yearbook of the Holocaust and Heroism, item by Elchanan Gafni–Brichah in Czechoslovakia, pp171–177. Published by Tel Itzhak, April 1997. No.25
33. Martin Smok– movie entitled Brichah
34. Toman file published by the office of the investigation of crimes committed under the Communist regime. Czech State documents. Baruch apparently refers to Bernard Baruch, a Jewish financial adviser to US presidents. He certainly was very familiar with the financial situation in the USA.
35. See Letter sent by Jacobson to New York October 11th, 1946

Chapter VIII
The Goldberger Family Reunites

Zdenek Toman was the first of the Goldbergers to reach liberated Prague. He was soon joined by his wife Pesla or Paula nee Gutman–Toman. On May 25th, 1945, a few days after the war ended, the Minister of Interior of Czechoslovakia, Vaclav Nosek, published a decree to the effect that Zdenek Toman was the head of the organization known as "Rozvedka" or secret service organization under the control of the Czech Communist Party. This organization later changed names but was always headed by Toman until his downfall in 1948. According to Igor Luke a western intelligence specialist on Czechoslovakia, Toman was an ardent communist devoted to rebuilding the party and its security apparatus[1]. Conditions were harsh in Czechoslovakia especially in the big cities. Food and medicines were in short supply and the black market flourished. Slowly, the country, which was flooded with thousands of survivors that were heading in all directions, started to solve its problems; the government helped the flow of refugees by establishing large camps and information offices.

Toman was soon informed that the entire Goldberger family had perished with the exception of himself and his older brother Armin who lived in Venezuela. Then news reached him that his sister Aranka or Aurelia Goldberger survived the camps and had reached Uzhhorod. He sent a car to bring her to Prague where she continued to recuperate. She then worked for the Ministry of Social Welfare where she met Imrich Rosenberg, an official of the repatriation commission within the Social Welfare Ministry. They married on October 2nd 1945 in accordance with Jewish law. The Rosenbergs rented their apartment to the Jacobsons and went on their honeymoon to Palestine. Rosenberg was very active in the Jewish community and in the Zionist movement. During the war he was in England and returned to liberated Czechoslovakia where he resumed his activities. He was a member of the repatriation office. The Jacobsons, Rosenbergs and the Tomans were very friendly and even met socially. The Tomans avoided publicity and were barely known in Prague but the name Toman created fear. Through his secret contacts, Toman soon discovered that another of his sisters survived the war. Lenke or Magdelena Goldberger was in a Swedish hospital where she was recuperating. Lenke was amongst a group of camp inmates that the Germans handed over to the Swedish Red Cross to care for them. All these survivors were transported to Swedish hospitals, amongst them Lenke Goldberger.

Lenke Goldberger was born in Sobrance, Slovakia to David and Rosalia nÉe Thoman. Her parents sent her to Fanny Thoman, a sister of Rosalia nÉe Thoman–Goldberger, who lived in Berlin Dahlen, at Kesserstrasse 21. In 1940, the Gestapo forced the Thomans to move to Berlin–Charlottenburg, Berliner Strasse 97 Berlin where they resided until September 1943. Fanny and her niece Lenke were then arrested and in October 1943 were sent to the Ravensbruck concentration camp. Fanny Thoman died at the camp on February 5th, 1945. Lenke was sent on a death march to Bergen Belsen. She reached the camp and collapsed. She managed to get herself included in a transport of sick inmates that were handed over to the Swedish Red Cross. Toman found her and brought her home to Prague. The Goldberger family was now reunited and slowly returning to a normal life.

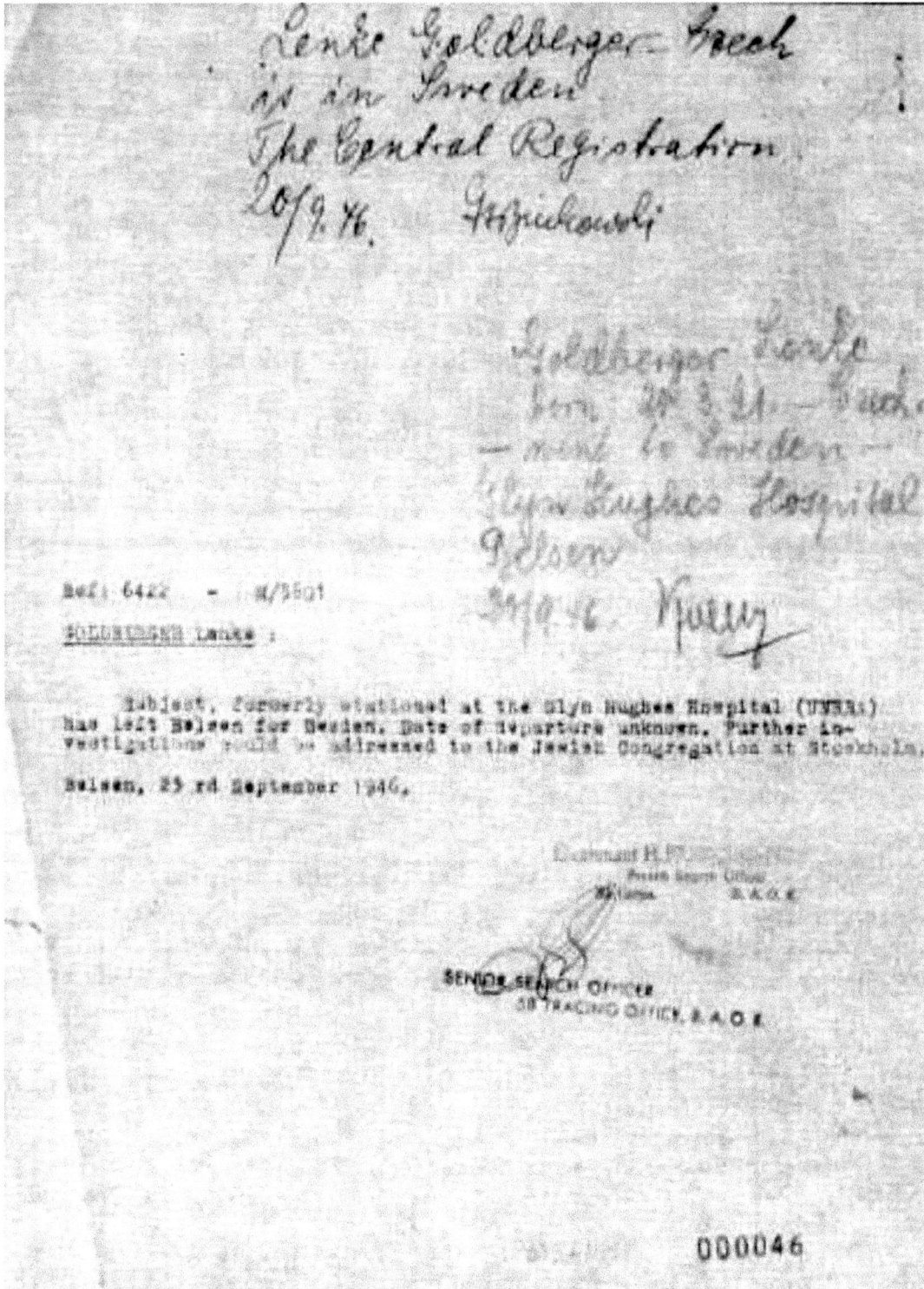

Tracing document indicates Lenke's whereabouts at the end of the war

Toman was very busy with the impending elections in Czechoslovakia. The Communist party waged an aggressive campaign to gain as many votes as possible. The campaign was hotly contested and showed an efficient Communist Party machinery that resulted in a smashing victory for the party. Of course Toman did his share of work in the campaign. Following the elections, the Czechoslovakian president asked Gottwald to form a government, which he did. Most key positions in the government were given to party members but other parties were represented in the government. The government functioned and Czechoslovakia slowly improved her economy. The government needed money to invest in the economy and money could only be gotten in the USA, where Masaryk hoped to raise money.

Toman did everything in his power to create a favorable American public opinion for Czechoslovakia. American Jewish and non-Jewish organizations were given free rein and they worked to help the Czech people and refugees. Jewish organizations established offices that handled Eastern Europe. The Jewish Agency headquarters in Eastern Europe were in Prague as were the offices of the Joint. The Joint operated the transit camps along the borders but also camps where the young Jews trained to become soldiers. The instructors were Palestinian Jews who were sent to train young Jews to fight for a Jewish Palestine.

The existence of these camps came to the forefront when the Soviets complained to Nosek that military training of Jews was taking place at some of the refugee camps.[2] Nosek asked Toman why he was not informed about the military training programs that included the use of weapons. Toman replied that he did not want to involve Nosek in this matter, but assured Nosek that there were no weapons in the camps, saying: "The Soviets can come any time to the camps and see for themselves that there are no weapons but they must give me prior notice of their visit.[3] Nosek told the Soviets to check the camps, which they did, but the Soviet NKVD found nothing. The latter complained to Nosek that somebody had removed or hidden the weapons. The NKVD knew that Toman was involved but decided not to make an issue of it at the time. Nosek warned Toman to be careful. The fact remained that the Haganah had an office in Prague that recruited young Jewish refugees. They were trained with weapons provided by the Interior Ministry, notably Toman.

He had contacts with the Haganah and the Mossad who were desperately trying to acquire weapons that were needed in Palestine where battles were taking place between Jews and Arabs. The Haganah and Mossad dispatched special agents to Prague to try to get some weapons, but without much success. These agents used every possible approach to get to Toman, who had the power to grant the necessary licenses to purchase weapons.

They approached Jacobson who interceded on their behalf with Toman. Czechoslovakia had a large military industry as well as huge stocks of light and heavy weapons that the German army had left in the country at the end of the war. The Haganah tried to purchase weapons for the expected battles in

Palestine but it was not very successful. One of the major problems was that most sellers feared British and American reprisals. Both countries were determined to prevent the shipping of weapons to the Jews in Palestine.

The Arabs could of course get or purchase weapons from the Arab countries. The suppliers also wanted hard cash and instant delivery. The Haganah could not purchase weapons and send them to Palestine in one shipment; the weapons had to be smuggled in small quantities, a long, tedious and costly process. Furthermore, the British secret services made sure that the arms dealers were forewarned not to sell weapons to the Jews. The Haganah agent in Czechoslovakia was Felix Doron or Felix Michael who decided to approach Toman via Jacobson. Doron was a native Czech speaker who studied at the Charles University and was familiar with many students who held high positions in the government and may have even known Toman in his student days. The Mossad agent in Prague was Ehud Avriel. Both agents pressed Toman to help the Jews acquire weapons. Toman presented the request to a meeting that included Gottwald, Nosek, Defense Minister General Ludwig Svoboda, the minister of defense and Toman himself[4]. Masaryk was also consulted on the deal. Moshe Sneh, member of the Jewish Agency was sent to Czechoslovakia by Ben– Gurion[5], head of the Jewish Agency for Palestine. He met Gottwald and stressed the need for the weapons and the certainty of payment. The committee hastily approved the sale of weapons to the Haganah before the Russians even had a chance to protest[6].

The Czechs approved the deal and orders were issued to permit the Haganah to purchase weapons. The technical arrangements were hastily processed by the assistance of Bedrich Reicin, assistant to the Czech defense minister[7]. Ehud Avriel in his book "*Open the Gates*" gives us a glimpse of the speed in which arms transactions took place[8]. In Paris Avriel met an agent named Robert Adam who was well connected with the Czech arms industry and both flew to Prague where arms deals were signed[9]. The first weapon deal was signed on January 10th 1948 and most of the weapons of this purchase reached Palestine on April 23rd 1948[10]. The first purchase would be followed by other arms purchases. This expanded, and included fighter planes, the training of fighter pilots, and the establishment of an Israeli air base at the Zatec airfield next to the East German border. This base would operate for several months: May – August 1948. Big American transport planes carried weapons and ammunition from Zatec airfield to Tel Aviv and returned empty[11]. These weapons proved to be crucial in the fight for Israel's survival.

Toman and Jacobson continued to handle the Jewish refugee transports that crossed the Czech borders, but the numbers began to decline as the number of Jewish survivors declined in Eastern Europe. The reservoir of Jewish manpower began to dry up. In accordance with the agreement between the Brichah and the Polish government, the period of open borders came to an end. The Czech–Polish borders were slowly sealed. Less and less Jews crossed these borders. Some Hungarian and Romanian Jewish transports continued to arrive and proceeded to the D.P. camps in Germany and Austria. The repatriation of Polish Jews from the Soviet Union reduced itself to a trickle. The Polish government slowly gained control of the country and established order. Jews could now apply to the Polish government and receive permits to leave the country. The other East European countries also seemed to stabilize their regimes and provide more security for the surviving Jews.

In June of 1945 there were about 60,000 Jewish survivors in Germany and Austria. By the middle of 1947 there were about 250,000 Jews in Germany and Austria and the numbers kept growing. These Jews built a new Jewish force that the world had to reckon with.

By August of 1947, the Jewish situation in Czechoslovakia had eased; few Jewish refugee transports crossed the country since the reservoir of potential Jewish refugees had steadily declined in Eastern Europe. The Jewish situation however in Hungary was desperate. Schwartz assigned Jacobson to head the Joint office in Budapest, Hungary. Jules Levine was sent to Prague to replace Jacobson. Toman was sad to see Jacobson go for they had worked together and accomplished so much for East European Jewry. They created a force that would fight Britain by any and all means: populate the illegal ships that would attempt to crash the British blockade of Palestine, mass demonstrations against Britain, boycotts of English products and last but not least put heavy pressure on American Jewry to act.

All these tactics had one goal: to open the gates of Palestine. Britain still refused to listen – instead decided to abandon Palestine altogether and hand over the country to the United Nations which established the State of Israel. Israel opened its gates and a mass exit of Jews from the D.P. camps ensued. Most of the Jewish refugees went to Palestine; almost all the camps in Germany, Austria, Italy, France and Belgium were eventually closed with the establishment of the State of Israel. In the new land, most of the refugees started a new, normal and productive life in an environment that accepted them and gave them hope and security.

The end of 1947 was indeed a very happy time for Zoltan Toman; his wife Pesla gave birth to a boy on October 4th 1947. The boy was named Ivan. The Goldberger family at last began to grow again in Czechoslovakia. Lenke, or Magdelena Goldberger–Thoman as she liked to be called, met and married Simon Leibovitz. The Goldberger families seemed to slowly emerge from the Shoah period and continue with their lives.

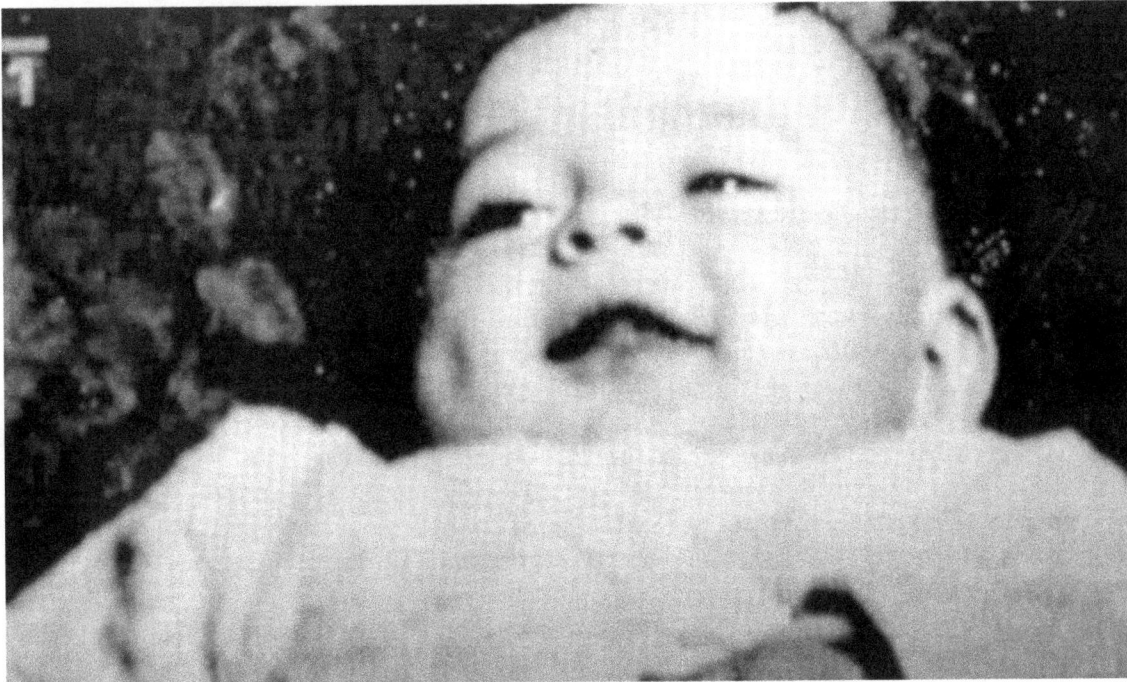

Ivan Toman, the son of Zdenek and Pesla Toman/Goldberger

Footnotes

1. Igor Lukas, *On the Edge of the Cold War*, Oxford Press, 2012, p.76
2. Tad Szulc, *Alliance*, p.156
3. Ibid p.156
4. Szulc, *Alliance*, p. 156.
5. Bauer. *Ashes*, p. 132.
6. Ibid p.156
7. He was born to a poor Jewish family by the name of Reinzinger. He joined the Communist Party in the thirties and in WWII served with the Czechoslovak Army under the command of Svoboda. Reicin also headed counter military intelligence. He would be shot later in Czechoslovakia.
8. Avriel, *Gates*. p.334
9. Ibid, p.334
10. A small amount of rifles and ammunition arrived by plane on April 3rd 1948. The big shipment arrived on April 23rd 1948 aboard the ship *Nora* from Yugoslavia. The shipment comprised 10,000 rifles, a number of machine guns and a large amount of ammunition. By October 1948, Czechoslovakia had sold 46751 rifles, 6142 machine guns of various types, 80 million rounds of ammunition and some fighter planes to Israel.
11. Most of the pilots were Jewish WWII war pilots and most of the planes were smuggled out of the USA.

Chapter IX
Toman's Downfall

In Eastern Europe new winds began to blow. Russia was having problems with Yugoslavia that refused to follow Stalin's political line. Marshal Tito in Yugoslavia and Stalin in Russia were at each other's throats, but Stalin could do little since there were no Russian troops in Yugoslavia. The pro–Russian elements in Yugoslavia were rounded up and disarmed. Tito was ready to fight and had the support of the West, namely the USA. Stalin had to accept defeat but decided to tighten control over his empire. The Russian secret services received orders to tighten controls in Eastern Europe. No more Tito–type situations. The various communist parties in Eastern Europe were told to prepare to take power in their countries. Fear and panic swept the communist world as the winds of the cold war progressed. Stalin's paranoia with Jews began to emerge into the open. Russian papers began to write anti–Jewish articles. The Jewish theater in Russia was being dismantled and the great Yiddish actor Salomon Michoels was banished to Minsk where he would be murdered. The Russian secret services received orders to begin to tighten their control in the satellite countries; even the NKVD in Prague was told to follow local events closely.

According to Toman's revelations at the American military base, the Czech Communist Party was ordered to prepare plans to seize power in Czechoslovakia. Furthermore, the Czech party was ordered to cooperate with the Soviet NKVD in Prague. The plotters began to draw plans and prepare lists of people that had to be removed from power, dismissed or jailed for the coup to succeed. One of the first to be eliminated would be Zdenek Toman. He was a Jew, well connected with Zionist and American organizations, lived for many years in England, and very independent and sure of himself in relation to the Russian secret service. The Soviet NKVD remembered Toman's acts of independence and was happy to settle scores with him. Gottwald and Slansky also wanted to rid themselves of Toman who was too involved in all kinds of financial and black market operations that provided money to the party apparatus and goods like perfumes to the wives of the party leaders[1]. Some communists were also happy to reduce his power. Toman was also very close to the Czech establishment, namely Jan Masaryk. His downfall had to be carried out very slowly but decisively since he controlled military forces, notably the border guards and other forces at his disposal in the Interior Ministry. The decision to destroy him was made in typical Stalinist fashion, namely he would be promoted to be Deputy Minister of the Interior. He lost control over the security forces to one of his subordinates in the fall of 1947[2]. Toman was neutralized by the move. As he himself told Tad Szulc, "I had access to all the files and knew what everybody did, so people were afraid of me." Toman still retained control of the Czech foreign intelligence services but his influence was on the decline, he was being pushed out of power. Nosek hinted to Toman that he would not be invited to the festivities at the Russian embassy party in honor of the Russian revolution, an event that was a must for all–important Czech communist officials.[3] Toman revealed some fears to his wife but she dismissed them. Toman was not invited to the party. The event encouraged his many opponents who, like sharks, smelled blood in the water. His wife Paula encouraged him to continue to build the new communist Czechoslovakia. Paula Toman was a devoted Communist Party member. Toman began to notice that his office was being ostracized by the Soviet NKVD. Even the Czech secret service organizations began to distance themselves from his offices.

Meanwhile the plotters began to look for people that could testify against Toman. It had to be people who knew Toman, worked with him and were intelligent. One of them would have to be the star witness around whom the entire case would be built. The team soon found Captain Adolf Puchler, a member of the Czech military intelligence. With the collapse of Czechoslovakia, Puchler managed to reach France and then England where he joined the free Czech forces in England. Toman met him there and they became friendly. Toman asked Puchler to join his secret services. Puchler was assigned to a post in London, where he was attached to the Czech diplomatic corps and was issued with a diplomatic passport. Puchler handled the diplomatic Czech courier between Prague and London. According to Puchler, he also transported jewelry in the diplomatic pouches that was sold on the black market in London. As a result of these activities, disagreements arose between the two men and Puchler wanted to leave his job but Toman refused to let him go. The implications were clear: Toman did not want Puchler to switch jobs and reveal the illegal financial operations. The plotters had an excellent witness who admitted that he committed crimes but also involved his boss.

Captain Adolf Puchler

Communist Czech leader Klement Gottwald addressing party members

According to Aranka Rosenberg, Puchler came to the office of her husband Imre Rosenberg and asked that all three go to Toman's office and convince him to return Puchler's diplomatic passport to him[4]. Toman refused to listen and told Puchler to leave his office. Puchler then threatened Toman that he would send a letter exposing him and his activities unless he received his diplomatic passport. He supposedly wanted to join his mistress Davidovitch in London. Toman refused to budge and Puchler made the following statement according to Aranka: "You are no longer the powerful man that you were." Toman saw the entrapment that Puchler represented. To grant a person a diplomatic document to meet his mistress was certainly a violation of the law of Czechoslovakia. Puchler then decided to send his letter to the secretary of the Czech Communist party, Rudolf Slansky.

General Secretary of the Czech Communist Party, Rudolf Slansky

Rudolf Slansky, General Secretary of the Czech Communist Party received the letter dated December 22, 1947 written by Adolf Puchler, a member of Toman's secret service organization.

Dokument č. 1

Dopis kpt. Adolfa Püchlera generálnímu tajemníkovi Ústředního sekretariátu KSČ Rudolfu Slánskému

Národní archiv, f. ÚV KSČ 100/36 (K. Šváb – H. Synková)

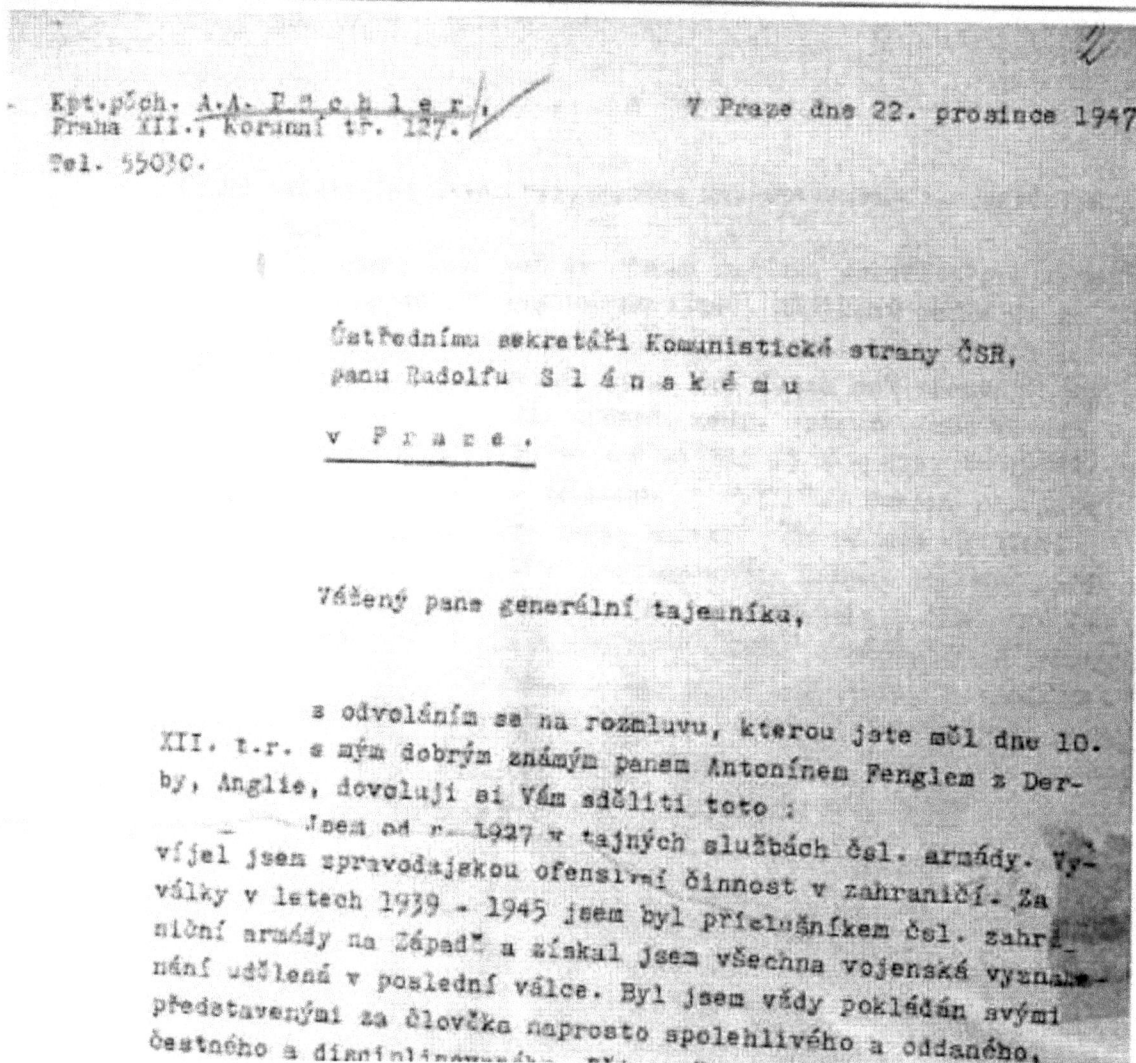

Kpt.pěch. A.A. P ü c h l e r,/   V Praze dne 22. prosince 1947
Praha XII., Korunní tř. 127./
Tel. 55030.

Ústřednímu sekretáři Komunistické strany ČSR,
panu Rudolfu S l á n s k é m u

v P r a z e .

Vážený pane generální tajemníku,

s odvoláním se na rozmluvu, kterou jste měl dne 10.
XII. t.r. s mým dobrým známým panem Antonínem Fenglem z Derby, Anglie, dovoluji si Vám sděliti toto :
Jsem od r. 1927 v tajných službách čsl. armády. Vy-
víjel jsem spravodajskou ofensivní činnost v zahraničí. Za
války v letech 1939 - 1945 jsem byl příslušníkem čsl. zahra_
niční armády na Západě a získal jsem všechna vojenská vyzna-
nání udělená v poslední válce. Byl jsem vždy pokládán svými
představenými za člověka naprosto spolehlivého a oddaného,
čestného a disciplinovaného,

The first page of Puchler's letter to Rudolf Slansky

Below translation of the Czech letter to English

Document Nr. 1
A Letter of Captain Adolf Puchler to the Secretary General of the Central Secretariat of the Czechoslovak Communist Party Rudolf Slansky
National Archives of the Central Committee of the Czechoslovak Communist Party. (K. Svab – H. Hynkova)

Prague, December 22th 1947
Captain of Army A.A. Puchler Prague, XII., Korunni Avenue 127 Tel………

To the Secretary General of the Czechoslovak Communist Party, Sir Rudolf Slansky

Prague.

Honorable Secretary General,

According to the discourse I had on December 10th with my good friend Sir Antonin Pengler from Derby, England, I allow myself to reveal to you the following information:

Since 1927 I have served with the Secret Service of the Czechoslovakian Army. I performed offensive intelligence activity abroad. During the war years 1939 – 1945 I was a member of the Czechoslovakian Army units in the West and was awarded military honors. I was always evaluated by my superiors as a fully reliable and loyal person, honest and disciplined. During the performance of these assigned tasks, I frequently risked my own life.

In September 1945 I was assigned at the request of the Ministry of Interior to the London Branch of this ministry. Since the day of my appointment I performed mainly investigatory tasks. In January 1946 I was assigned by my chief, Doctor Toman, to perform other jobs too, connected to financial matters. Doctor Toman informed me that these activities were official and served the Czech Communist Party. I was also told not to ask questions but to execute the orders. As a disciplined intelligence agent I performed these assignments exactly as ordered. I never asked Doctor Toman for details. I frequently traveled between London and Prague with a special diplomatic passport.

On April 1, 1946 I was ordered by Dr. Toman to raise –50.000 English pounds to buy Czech bijouterie or jewelry that would be transported to England and sold on the black market. Doctor Toman told me clearly that it was in the interests of the Czechoslovak Communist Party and the Interior Ministry. He promised me 25% from the net profit, as a special reward. I was ordered by Doctor Toman to contact the head of the army headquarters General Bocek, to obtain a courier letter from him. Doctor Toman knew that I had good relations with General Bocek, and indeed he obtained the courier letter for me without asking for details or explanations. I alone had to organize the transfer of the bijouterie to England. I obtained the financial resources needed for purchasing the bijouterie partly from Doctor Toman directly – 450.000 Czech crowns, and partly by selling my foreign currency deposits that I had sent to England in 1939. I was then to sell the jewelry in England and bring back English pounds that would be sold on the local Czech market at a tremendous profit. I purchased the jewelry according to these orders. Before leaving for England Doctor Toman asked for his money of 450.000 Czech crowns. He informed me that he expected an imminent inspection by Major Pokorny, head of the Intelligence Department of the Ministry of Interior. I told Doctor Toman that the money had been used for the purchase of the jewelry. Doctor Toman demanded categorically that I return his money and ignored my protests that I had no money to give him. He then advised me to borrow money from my acquaintances in Czechoslovakia and to promise them that I would open Sterling accounts in England for them. People would thus send money abroad without paying taxes or duties, a highly illegal act. I acted according to his suggestions, I found people interested in illegal transfer of Czech crowns to England and getting British Pounds. I obtained 450.000 Czech crowns and turned them over to Doctor Toman. I transferred the jewelry to England where it was sold illegally. The money was brought back to Czechoslovakia in English pounds and distributed. I personally gave Doctor Toman 3,500 English pounds in July or August 1946 in profit money.

During his stay in London Doctor Toman tried to sell some photo cameras. I had an appointment with him at the Hyde Park Hotel, where he appeared in the company of a person unknown to me. He left this person in the lobby and told me that he got acquainted with him in a shop in the Strand and this man was interested in buying the cameras. On seeing the party, I immediately began to suspect that he was a British agent. I advised Doctor Toman to tell him that he could only sell the cameras after paying customs tax. The cameras were brought to England by Toman in the diplomatic luggage. I got the impression that the

English customs officers and security services were suspicious of Czechoslovakian officials and shadowed them. To this day, I don't know how Toman sold the cameras.

In 1946 I executed a number of similar actions that were ordered by Doctor Toman. I purchased jewelry in Czechoslovakia, transferred it in diplomatic pouches to London, where I sold it on the black market for sterling. In the autumn of 1946, I don't remember the exact date, Doctor Toman asked me to withdraw 8,000 English pounds from the Czech treasury on behalf of Mrs. Toman for her journey to London. On receiving the money, I handed it over to Mrs. Toman. Doctor Toman urged me in Hungarian to seal the package containing the money with a special seal and not to reveal the contents of the package to Mrs. Toman. I took the precaution and wrote down all the serial numbers of the British pounds. A few days later I was asked by Mrs. Toman to help her purchase clothing fabrics in London at Rudinger Company on Regent Street 335, and at the Hartman Company on Bond Street. She gave me a bundle of B#1 notes to pay the bill. I identified these notes as the same notes that I handed her in the sealed parcel and I recognized their numbers.

I returned to Prague prior to Christmas 1946. Not all the business transactions were closed, since I still had part of the jewelry in London where I also had #10,000 in the office vault. In Prague Doctor Toman asked me to immediately raise 1,000,000 Czech crowns for him. I obtained this amount from Czech citizens as loans against my promise to get English pounds for them and deposit the money in their accounts in England."

The charge letter continued to describe financial deals and cash transactions that were ordered by Doctor Toman and executed by Puchler. No supporting evidence was enclosed with the letter.

Then the letter turned to matters of state.

"In 1948 Toman participated in activities to the detriment of the state. He kept contacts with enemies of the state such as Ladislav Prchala, Chairman of the so–called Czech National Committee for Western Europe, and Mirko Cerny, a member of the same enemy organization. He passed information about the Czech defense intelligence services, to them and to other similar persons particularly the names of the agents that would affect the security of the nation. The release of this information would weaken the Czech defense apparatus.

Aurelie Rosenberg, being related to the head of the Intelligence Department of the Ministry of Interior, Zdenek Toman, extracted information from him regarding military intelligence information and passed it on to people that worked for organizations that were inimical to the State of Czechoslovakia. She passed on military intelligence information to people like Dr. Imrich Rosenberg who worked for Ladislav Prchala, and thus participated in enemy activities aimed at our country, with the objective of destroying our people's democratic regime by force.

So all of them, together with additional people, conspired and contacted directly or eventually indirectly with enemy powers, who sent foreign military activists to damage the republic, with the aim of violently changing the constitution of the republic, mainly its independence, unity and the people's democratic form of the state, and these activities were carried out during the very important period of the building of the republic, the people's democratic regime, in a time that demanded tranquility, and in the period the republic was being threatened by organized activities of the reactionary forces from inside and from abroad, that were in very grave circumstances...

They disclosed directly, eventually indirectly to the enemy powers, issues that were not to be disclosed being that they were important to the defense of the republic, and their activities were dangerous since they revealed state secrets.

Doctor Zdenek Toman was sworn to secrecy due to his position as a chairman of an important department of the Ministry of Interior in Prague. In the years 1946 and 1947 he conducted personal illegal business activities, which could damage the credibility of the republic abroad, by smuggling bijouterie and other high–value items in diplomatic luggage to Great Britain.

In 1947 Doctor Toman obtained from M.... (unreadable–I.H.) /Abraham K.... (unreadable)/ big amounts of money that led to the release of K, a former Jewish head of the Ostrowce Jewish concentration camp. He was a war criminal and was arrested by the Czech authorities. He was released by Toman who used his power as an official by damaging the state interests."

The letter in essence outlined the case against Toman. No other high official was involved. Toman functioned in a vacuum. He bought and sold jewelry to make money which he did not spend. His style of living was very modest. Notice that the letter does not say that he entertained lavishly or had big expenses. The letter goes on with imaginary acts of wrong doing when in reality the communist party was the one that seized power illegally and destroyed the Czech Republic.

The letter goes on and lists a variety of illegal operations that Puchler performed for Toman. Most of these operations were illegal and supposedly served Toman. The basic charge was the smuggling of jewelry and selling it on the black market in England. The letter demands action.

The letter should have been sent to the Minister of Justice, Dr. Ortina or to the Minister of Interior in charge of police matters, Nosek or the Minister of Defense, General Svoboda. Instead Puchler send his accusation letter to the Secretary of the Czechoslovak Communist Party, Rudolf Slansky. The latter was not a member of the government and held no official position in the Czech administration. Receiving such a letter was a crime in itself since Slansky was not authorized to receive or handle state security matters. Slansky showed the letter to Gottwald as planned. The latter presented the document to the government or the cabinet. They had decided on a plan of action. Both Czech communist leaders were under pressure from Moscow to move ahead with the seizure of power in Czechoslovakia. Gottwald and Slansky apparently set up a closed committee within the central party committee to co-ordinate activities with the Russian and Czech security services handling the case. This was no ordinary investigation. This involved an important and powerful member of the communist party. The findings would have to be presented at the right time to the Czech Central Committee for action. Both Czech communist leaders knew that they would soon seize power and then dispose of the case of Toman. The investigation had to be conducted in a highly secretive manner in order not to provide ammunition to the anti-communist forces. The fact that the communist party was involved in plotting to seize power was another reason for total secrecy.

Toman was accused of betraying the interest of the country by revealing secrets to foreign countries. Basically, the letter accused Toman of being interested in money. An accusation that would be hurled against many Jewish communists in future trials. Of course, London was picked as the center of all illegal activities since Toman, Puchler and Rosenberg spent the war years in England. The fact that Britain disliked Toman and did everything in its power to remove him from his post for allowing the Jews of Eastern Europe to cross Czechoslovakia never entered the case. British secret services were closely watching all the activities of Toman's agents in England and would have loved to expose or compromise Toman in such an affair. The fact that no such event occurred gave little credence to the smuggling stories. Even the CIA records noted the anti-British feelings of Toman. But logic and facts aside, Stalin had decided to finish Toman.

Slansky and Gottwald began to execute the order. The letter was the first actual step in the destruction of Toman. The search began to find incriminating evidence against Toman. The findings were known in advance. Toman must be found guilty. Rumors and innuendoes were collected and entered in the file. Supposedly huge profits were made and the money supported the Czech Communist Party and also some officials of the party or their wives received beautiful gifts[5]. We know from Aranka's and Toman's testimony that the Tomans had few friends and barely mingled in Czech society due to his position. Toman himself stated that he never made speeches or participated in public debates. People knew of him but not him. The mere mention of his name or office was enough to discourage people from approaching him.

Toman was very busy and began to stay at his office at night. According to Aranka, her brother hardly came home and there was a lack of food in the house. She criticized him for the situation at the house and she herself brought food to the family from her own house and tried to help Paula and the baby with their needs. Meanwhile, the Czech security found enough evidence to make a case against Toman. The evidence was presented to Slansky and Gottwald who presented it to the Czech Central Committee.

The latter approved the arrest of Toman that was issued on January 28 1948. The execution of the act was delayed since the Czech communist party was involved in the final preparations to seize power in Czechoslovakia and decided to postpone Toman's arrest. On February 25th 1948, the Czech communists seized power in the country. Within two weeks, on March 10, 1948 Jan Masaryk, beloved Czech leader, supposedly committed suicide by falling out the window of his office. The Czechs were bewildered by the rapidity of events. They saw their country slip into the orbit of the communist world. Rapid changes took place overnight, border controls were closed, non–party officials were arrested or dismissed en masse, unreliable officials were sent home or arrested, and many people, including Jews, immediately left the country. An arrest warrant was issued against Imre Rosenberg on March 23, 1948[6]. But Rosenberg was tipped off and left the country in a hurry, first to Brussels supposedly on a mission for a Czech business company; he decided to extend his stay in Belgium and then left for London.[7] He wrote to his wife that he was very busy and would soon return home to Prague. Aranka was a bit worried by his absence and spoke to her brother regarding Imre Rosenberg. He of course assured her that everything would be fine. The secret service never bothered to question Aranka about the whereabouts of her husband. The secret service did visit the Rosenberg family in Nove Mesto and asked questions. According to Menachem Rosenberg, a nephew of Imre, the police visited the Rosenberg home several times and even arrested Abraham Rosenberg, the brother of Imre. He was kept in jail but was released, since it became obvious that he knew very little about Imre's business activities. The two brothers maintained a distant relationship. Abraham survived the Holocaust in the camps and returned to his furniture store in Nove Mesto while Imre lived in Prague and led a very busy political life. Abraham did not know too much about Imre's whereabouts or activities[8]. As the days passed Aranka became more concerned and spent more of her time with Paula Toman and the baby. Lenke and Simon Lebovitc also managed to leave Czechoslovakia. The Czech and Russian secret services began to suspect that someone was dismantling their case, for important people that were essential to the case began to disappear, notably Rosenberg whose name appeared in Puchler's accusation letter. The secret service began to fear that Toman would also disappear. The Interior Minister, Nosek was ordered to place Toman in a maximum security place, a so–called rest home in total isolation. The order was immediately carried out and Toman was quietly whisked off to his isolation without even saying good bye to his wife and baby.

Toman was kept in isolation while the communists consolidated themselves in power. Most of the non–party officials were purged, even some party officials that were independent, were dismissed. Paula did not know what happened. Aranka urged her to see Nosek and talk to him about Toman[9]. She saw Nosek and asked him what had happened to her husband. He assured her that he was fine but needed absolute rest and isolation. He told her that he would soon be home. Shortly thereafter Toman was sent home. In March of 1948 Imre Rosenberg arrived in London, where he started to contact people notably Zionist organizations regarding help to get his wife Aranka out of Czechoslovakia. This proved very difficult since the Czechs were looking for him and already checked the Rosenberg family in Czechoslovakia. All his attempts to get Aranka out of Czechoslovakia failed. He decided to head to Canada where he was naturalized in 1954.

The Toman family was very happy to see Toman home after a lengthy absence. He rested for a few days and then headed to his office. A few days later, on April 27th 1948, he was arrested at 10.40 in the morning in his office. He was not presented with a charge sheet nor informed of his crimes. His sister Aranka Rosenberg–Goldberg was arrested on April 28, 1948 at 8.40 in the morning. She too was not shown a charge sheet or formal arrest order. At that moment she was not even employed, having been dismissed from her job at the social services some time earlier. In all likelihood they decided to arrest her to ensure her presence in the country and at the forthcoming trial of Zdenek Toman.

Footnotes

1. Lukes, Journal, pp18–19
2. The Czeck police charge sheet.
3. Toman's letter to Ben Gurion University dated 12/3/1982
4. Aranka's testimony at her trial in Prague.
5. Lukes, *Journal*, pp18–19
6. Czech records and Aranka Goldberger testimony.
7. Menachem Rosenberg, Imre's nephew.
8. Ibid.
9. Aranka testimony at her trial

Chapter X
The Escape

Toman was taken to a small jail in the Justice Palace building that was located near Charles Square instead of the highly congested prison of Pancrac. We have to remember that the Communist regime arrested many people, and the jails and penal institutions were very crowded. The atmosphere in the palace jail was relaxed and the detainees were permitted to use the phone to call family or friends. Later police interrogations established that one of the guards mailed some letters for Toman[1]. Toman was constantly interrogated but kept his civilian clothing. Naturally, he told the interrogators that a terrible mistake had been made and he expected to be released at any moment. This bravado stance did not prevent him from hearing rumors in the jail that he would be hanged.

On May 8, 1948 the Czech police received a telephone call from a building janitor who said that a woman had fallen to her death from his building and her body was lying in his courtyard.

An entire team of police officials and medical doctors was sent to the scene where they confirmed that the person was dead. The police said that the body was that of Pesla Gutman–Toman who had supposedly committed suicide. A letter was found in her handbag addressed to Captain Jiri Vesely, a high security official, asking him to take her child and raise him to be a good Communist. There were also 150 Czech korunas in her bag. Pesla Toman's body was removed to the police mortuary where an autopsy was performed that confirmed she had committed suicide. She was cremated and the urn containing her ashes was kept by the crematorium with specific orders not to release it without consulting the security police The death was never published in the press or reported on the radio. No police investigation was conducted nor were neighbors questioned as to what happened. The baby Ivan Toman was placed at the Stvanice shelter for children[2]. The baby was placed in a state shelter although Pesla had a brother in Czechoslovakia according to Aranka. He visited Aranka in jail, and later left for Israel.

The entire situation surrounding Pesla's death was bizarre, to say the least. She was a devoted Communist and refused to believe the suspicions that her husband had offered lately about his situation. She believed in the so–called "New Czechoslovakia". Then suddenly her husband disappears, is kept in isolation, released and finally arrested. Secret service agents begin to visit her apartment and apparently pressure her to cooperate with the investigation. She of course knows very little if anything, but the agents are not interested in what she knew or did not know; they want her to sign papers and/or participate in the show trial. Presently they are talking but she knows that the talk could turn ugly. She is alone, Aranka is in jail and so is her husband Zdenek. Both are far away and cannot be reached. She has nobody with whom to discuss things. She is basically alone and under a great deal of pressure. So was her husband.

Toman was also familiar with the Russian communist trials and knew that his chances of survival were slim. He began planning his escape and wrote many letters to his friends and acquaintances that he helped in time of need, pleading with them to help him. He wrote many letters that were carried out of jail and mailed by Sedlacek, a security officer with the Czech National Security or SNB (Statni Narodna Bezchnost)[3]. Perhaps the unofficial courier also brought back replies to him. The police interrogations later revealed that Toman enlisted the aid of Sedlacek a member of the SNB (Statni Narodna Bezchnost) or National Security Office to send letters and probably receive mail from the outside[4]. Some of the letters were even written in Hungarian to his acquaintance Dr. Golan whom he had helped in the past. Golan worked for the Magnet Company connected to the Interior Ministry. Toman begged for help. Golan kept the contents of the letter to himself and then spoke to Dr. Junger who also received a similar letter. Both discussed the matter and turned Toman down. Golan even verbally reported the contents of the letters to the authorities. On June 16, 1948, Police Inspector Pokorny ordered the arrest of Agent Sedlacek, Golan and Junger and other people related to the case.

Pesla's death shocked Toman and showed him that the Czech and Russian secret services meant business and expected full cooperation in their planned scenario. This was going to be a big show to detract the people's attention from their daily life in Communist Czechoslovakia. They lost some potential defendants but they planned to get some star witnesses to fill the gap. But their plan was undermined by the disappearing witnesses, and the death of Pesla Toman was a serious blow to the case. The proceedings were very slow. The plotters took their sweet time to prepare the show trial. Other rescue letters were sent to other people and were turned down. The American embassy in Prague also said 'no' – with an attachment: 'to contact us when you are out of Czechoslovakia[5].' The British were not even asked for help, but some letters reached the right people. Apparently Jacobson received a letter.

In August of 1947, Jacobson had been appointed to head the Joint organization in Hungary. The Hungarian Jews were in a terrible situation. Almost 50,000 elderly Jews had no means of support. The total Jewish population was about 200,000 of whom 50,000 lived in the provinces and the rest in Budapest[6]. The UNRRA was not permitted to function in Hungary nor were other Western aid organizations. The Joint was the only organization to help the Jews in Hungary. The Joint also helped non–Jewish institutions. Hungary prevented Jews from leaving the country but the local Brichah managed to get some Jews out of the country. The Joint actively supported the Jewish community and according to Jacobson "we had soup kitchens for singles, soup kitchens for families, and we had a soup kitchen that served starving Hungarian artists, writers, poets and actors that were mainly non–Jewish"[7]. Jacobson became friendly with Matyas Rakosi, General Secretary of the Hungarian Communist Party. He was probably the only westerner to have such an access in Hungary. Jacobson was also familiar with other communist leaders like Laszlo Rajk, the Interior Minister.

On receiving Toman's letter, Jacobson realized the seriousness of the situation. Toman knew a great deal of information about him, the Joint, the various manipulations that dealt with transporting the Jews across Czechoslovakia, transporting Soviet Jews out of the area of Carpatho–Russia, helping Soviet Jews like the Lubavicher Hasidim cross Czechoslovakia etc.

Under torture, these things would probably come out and destroy Jacobson and probably the Joint activities in Eastern Europe. He had to take steps to help Toman escape. Jacobson had a diplomatic passport that enabled him to travel freely across the borders. He also had access to American dollars and American cigarettes worth their weight in gold in postwar Europe. Toman apparently also contacted the Mossad office in Prague which contacted the head of the organization in Israel, Shaul Avigur. The latter, like Jacobson, did not want revelations of Mossad's dealings with Toman. He also knew that the Israeli government was negotiating various arm deals with the Czech government that Toman had initiated. Exposure of these negotiations would harm the Israeli army that needed weapons badly. Both parties decided to act to get Toman out of jail.

Jacobson often visited Prague and was very familiar with the city, where he had excellent contacts. The Brichah organization was being dismantled with the establishment of the State of Israel but there were still enough Mossad and Brichah agents in Prague to assist Jacobson with the operation. Jacobson visited Prague several times prior to the escape. As a matter of fact, he was in Prague the day of the escape but did not stop at the Joint office in Prague. Furthermore some Czech officials were more than happy to be bribed to help Toman's escape for they felt threatened enough by his arrest that they were willing to help the escape plan. The plan, of course worked like a charm.

On June 23, 1948, the signal was given to launch the operation. Toman was cleaning the jail's lavatories when he suddenly locked the door of the lavatory from the inside. He freshened up and changed some clothes that he had been wearing since his arrest. He dressed and went to one of the windows and lowered himself to a balcony that led to a large hall. He entered the hall, tall and erect, saluted some officers and continued to walk. He left the jail and entered a waiting vehicle, disappearing from sight within seconds. Toman was driven to a secret hiding place out of town. He was told to stay put until his rescuers arrived for him. Most of the major participants including Jacobson left Prague the same day. Thus, there were no traces and no clues.

Toman did not need lessons in hiding. He was very familiar with police procedures in such cases. He was aware that he must stay underground or he would be spotted and reported to the police. Meanwhile, inmates tried to use the lavatory and found it locked. They banged on the door but got no response. The janitor was called and he forced the door open. Nobody was there except for the cleaning tools. The alarm was sounded. All inmates were sent to their cells. Rosters were checked and rechecked; Toman was missing. The event was immediately reported to Nosek who reported it to Slansky and Gottwald. Police and army units were ordered to establish road blocks throughout the city. The area where Toman lived was surrounded by the police and searches were conducted throughout the neighborhood. Toman's picture was circulated amongst the police. Agents were ordered to patrol the streets to look for Toman. Hours passed and days passed and still no Toman. Slansky was furious. He revealed to some members of the central committee that Toman knew a great deal of state secrets. The Soviet NKVD was livid. They had to report to Moscow that Toman had escaped from jail. To raise the moral of the secret services, the Czech secret services released rumors that Anglo–American imperialist agents helped Toman escape but he would never leave the country. He would be apprehended. The security forces were ordered to place tight security at the entrances of foreign embassies and western agencies like the Joint offices.

Mass arrests of guards took place, relatives of the guards were arrested, people that worked with Toman were arrested and still no leads. In a letter to the Joint in New York, Julius Levine, director of the Joint in Prague states that his personal driver, a Mr. Spits, was arrested on June 24, 1948 at 3.30 in the morning and was questioned until 7.30 and then released[8]. His apartment was searched. He was again arrested later in the day. The Czech police wanted to know some details about the use of Joint cars. It appears that a particular car of the Joint was seen in front of the Toman residence some months earlier. The letter mentions that Jacobson had arrived in Prague from Budapest on June 16, 1948 and spent the night there. On June 17, 1948, Jacobson visited Levine at the Joint office in Prague and they discussed the Toman situation. Jacobson then left for Zurich, Switzerland. On June 23, 1948 Jacobson passed through Prague on his return to Hungary[9]. Levine himself was invited to visit the police station where he was questioned mostly about his relationship with Toman and Rosenberg. He was also asked about Jacobson's relations with the Tomans and the Rosenbergs. The Joint director was then informed that the Czech authorities were of the opinion that the Joint was involved in the escape. They expressed a desire to question Jacobson who was no longer in Prague but in Budapest. Levine informed Jacobson that the Czechs wanted to talk to him. Levine urged Jacobson to come to Prague and talk to the police. Levine reasoned that the Czech police only wanted to talk to Jacobson. The latter took Levine's advice and went to Prague where he was arrested on arrival at the airport. He was taken to prison and interrogated for many days about Toman's escape. He was lucky and managed to leave the prison and head directly to the American embassy in Prague. The American ambassador immediately made arrangements for his departure. He was taken directly to the airport and boarded a plane for Budapest where he resumed the Joint activities of helping the Jewish population and assisting the Brichah in taking Jews out of Hungary. These operations became more difficult as the days passed. The Cold War intensified and the Hungarian authorities followed the Russian line. Eventually Jacobson was arrested and interrogated. He was forced to leave the country[10]. The Hungarians also closed down the Joint offices in the country.

Group of Zionist youth members leave Hungary with the help of the Hungarian Brichah

Toman was still in hiding and lived on bread and onions according to Szulc who interviewed him[11]. Szulc also reports that Toman supposedly went to the house of Levine following his escape from jail in order to get help but Levine refused to help him. Szulc also reported that Toman obtained a passport and took the train to the German border, which he crossed and reached the West German hamlet of Ash. These stories are an attempt to confuse and mislead the reader. We already mentioned that Prague was bristling with police forces that checked everybody and everything, notably the homes of Westerners. Yet Szulc wants us to believe that Toman was strolling through the streets of Prague looking for help – hardly likely! Toman did not take the train since they were tightly controlled, especially those heading to the German border. The borders were closed and people arriving near the border were thoroughly checked and rechecked.

False identity papers were prepared for Toman and he was removed from his hiding place and probably driven to the border where professionals took him across the border near the hamlet of Ash in West Germany. The area was the main crossing point for Jews leaving Czechoslovakia and entering the American zone in Germany. On entering Germany Toman proceed to the first American military establishment and requested political asylum[12]. Toman knew that the Czech and Russian secret services were looking for him, as well as the various Czech Nationalist groups that would have liked to get their hands on him. He therefore decided to procure his safety by placing himself in American hands. According to the American military intelligence records he was flown to Camp King located near Oberursel near Frankfurt– am–Main, Germany. This post was a major debriefing place for defectors from the Soviet bloc. Apparently Toman insisted on a passport and visa to Venezuela where his brother Armin Goldberger lived. He also demanded transportation and safe passage to Venezuela. South American governments, notably Venezuela, were reluctant to grant visas to Jewish refugees. The fact that Toman was a high Communist official in the Czech government made the situation worse. South America was terrified of communists especially Jewish communists.

Brichah leaders in Hungary in 1947

Seated: **Itzhak Ayalon and Blatberg**
Standing from left: **Yossef Reissman, Moshe Breitbart, Shlomo Haft, Moshe Podor (Amir Doron)**

The entire Toman story was of course widely publicized when the Czech government published a request through Interpol for help in locating Zdenek Toman who had committed serious crimes against the state. The request appealed to all countries to help arrest the former Czech official Toman, and send him back to Czechoslovakia to be brought to justice and stand trial

Toman provided the Americans with information regarding the preparations and execution of the plan to seize power. He explained that Russia pressed the reluctant Czech Communist leaders to act. Slansky and Gottwald hesitated; they were comfortable with the existing Czech political situation that depended on their support. Both Czech leaders knew that seizing power would abolish the existing political system. Stalin insisted on action according to Toman in his revelations to the American intelligence. As the Cold War progressed and intensified, Stalin wanted full control of his satellites. He had no intention of repeating the Yugoslav mistake where he permitted Tito to escape his hegemony. The fact that Russia had no military forces in Yugoslavia enabled Tito to seize power and arrest all pro–Soviet elements in the country. Stalin was determined not to repeat the same mistake. He insisted on action. Toman also provided a picture of the members of the Central Czech Committee and their interrelations. The Americans received pages of information regarding the preparations, the implementations and the actual seizure of power. Toman was also very familiar with the workings of the Russian secret service in Czechoslovakia and abroad. He was able to provide the scope of Russian–Czech penetration into Western society. Toman was an important catch for the Americans since he provided many keys to the Czech and Russian espionage systems. Of course Toman was always aware that his son was being held by the Czechs and he had to play a careful game. This fact was also known to the Americans.

Footnotes

1. Czech police investigation report.
2. Police report of Pesla/Paula Gutman–Toman
3. Protocol of Aranka's testimony in jail
4. Police report on the arrested guards at the jail house
5. Lukas, Czechoslovakia, pp. 18–20
6. Szulc, Alliance p.177
7. Szulc, Alliance p.180
8. Letter dated July 2, 1948 sent by Julius Levine in Prague to M.W. Beckelman in Paris.
9. Ibid.
10. Szulc, Alliance pp.199–202
11. Szulc, Alliance pp. 195–196
12. Lukes, Journal. pp. 18–20

Chapter XI
The Trial

The debriefing finished, Toman was flown from Frankfurt Germany to Paris, France. He called Nosek from Paris and wanted to know how his son was doing. Nosek told him to keep quiet and no harm would come to his son. He also inquired about his sister and was told not to worry. Toman was then flown to Argentina and on to Venezuela where his brother's family awaited him. His sister Aranka was in the Pancrak jail since her arrest on April 28th, 1948. It was decided to arrest her to insure that she remained in Czechoslovakia, because too many people involved in the case had disappeared. Aranka never held an important position nor was she an influential figure in Czechoslovakia. She was not expected to be a star witness but merely 'another' witness. According to Aranka, Joe Rosenberg, her uncle, visited her in May of 1948 in prison and told her that he had just spoken to the officer in charge of the investigation, Pokorny, who told him that Aranka was just a security arrest to influence other witnesses in the case and she would soon be released to rejoin her husband abroad[1]. All this changed radically with Toman's escape.

Suddenly she became the only member of the family in Czechoslovakia. The entire case rested on Aranka. Obviously the idea of the great public show trial had to be dropped. The plotters decided to try the case behind closed doors. Prague had to show Moscow that they were doing something. Aranka was frequently questioned, notably about Toman's escape. She was of course watched very carefully. She was the only party left in the entire case. Still she was interrogated regarding her brother's escape. See some of the questions and answers provided by Aranka[2].

In her testimony Aranka states that her brother–in–law Kadlac told her that Toman was hiding with Dr. Banar. Then she dismisses the suggestion by stating that the two were not exactly friends. Kadlac lists the people that might have helped Toman, namely Nosek, Jacobson, Eva Elefantova who worked for the Jewish organization in Bratislava, and Dr. Sobicka from the American embassy in Prague. All names were possibilities but no individual could carry out such an extensive operation by himself. The escape required a detailed plan that involved several phases and several people. Of course, Aranka did not know a thing about the escape since she was sitting in jail when the escape took place. Furthermore, Toman would never have told her the details unless she was involved in the plan. Yet, the Czech interrogators kept asking her about Toman's escape, and she gave the same laconic answers. Basically, she did not know a thing about the escape except for the fact that it had taken place.

Below are excerpts of Aranka's interrogations;

Question directed to Aranka.

What is the meaning of your brother–in–law's statement that Interior Minister Vaclav Nosek was committed to Zdenek Toman?

Aranka:

"In March of 1948, Toman was sent to a health farm to rest. His wife Pesla/Paula was very worried by his absence. She went to Nosek and asked and asked about her husband. Nosek assured her that Toman was fine but needed some rest. He told her that Toman would soon be sent home and would be in charge of the fund for the national renewal. Paula confided to me that half the furniture in Nosek's apartment belonged to the Renewal Minister."

Question directed to Aranka.

What do you know about Zdenek Toman's escape?

Aranka:

"My husband Immerich Rosenberg was friendly with Captain Adolf Puchler who worked for the Interior Ministry. As a matter of fact, we socialized with Puchler. Towards the end of 1947 or the beginning of 1948, Puchler came to see my husband, who worked for a private finance company, in his office. He asked Immerich and myself to go to Toman's office. Puchler said that maybe the three of us could convince Toman to give Puchler back his passport. Apparently Toman refused to return it. My husband and I refused to involve ourselves in the situation. Puchler then stated that he had already written out a complaint against Toman's behavior. Furthermore, he said that he would not post the letter if Toman would return his diplomatic passport so that he could join his mistress in London. We stood our ground and Puchler shouted that Toman was no longer the strong man in the ministry. He then turned to the office entrance where Pokorny and Triskolova, two secret agents, stood and said 'They want me to file the complaint so that they could arrest Toman. The agents promised me that they would return my passport if I cooperated.'"

These type of interrogations repeated themselves until the trial of Aranka. Aranka was a survivor of the German concentration camps so prison life was no novelty for her.

a vérification de nos archives a permis de relever les éléments suivants :

Lenka/Magdalena DE LEBIVIC, née GOLDBERGER
le 20.1.1913 à Sobrance (Tchécoslovaquie), noms des
parents : David et Rosa, née THOMAN.

habitait en décembre 1959 au Venezuela, Caracas, Apart 9215.

Dans le cadre de nos recherches, les informations ci-après nous ont été
uquées :

Le dernier courrier contenu dans le dossier date de 1971. Madame Toman-
ger de Lebowic est manifestement décédée à une date ultérieure. Elle a émigré er
Venezuela. La dernière adresse en ma possession est la suivante : San Bernadine
uiso Edif. Ofelia Ap. 5, Venezuela. Madame Toman-Goldberger de Lebowic étau
rvec Monsieur Simon Lebovic. Je ne sais pas si des enfants sont issus de ce
Le dossier fait état des noms suivants : Armin Goldberger de Caracas/Venezuel
homan de Caracas et Aurelia Rozmeuk de Caracas (tous sans indication de date
ance) Les liens de parenté ne ressortent pas clairement du dossier.

Vous nous permettons de solliciter votre assistance dans cette affaire et vous prion
faire savoir s'il vous est possible de recueillir des renseignements sur le sort de
: Toman-Goldberger de Lebowic, et de retrouver la trace d'éventuels parents
habitant au Venezuela, qui seraient intéressés à une prise de contact avec Monsie
Staadt.

Nous vous remercions à l'avance de vos efforts et attendons votre réponse avec

Veuillez agréer, Messieurs, l'expression de nos salutations distinguées

S. Gutzeit
pour les archives

**Letter sent by the Venezuelan Red Cross in French to the Berlin organization that
tried to locate Thoman survivors to honor them**

Toman left Paris, France and headed to Argentina and then to Caracas, Venezuela where the Goldberg family awaited. His older brother Armin Goldberger, his wife Suze, his son Thomas and daughter Mazaal were very happy to see him. They were later joined by Lenke Goldberger, now Lenke Goldberger–Lebovic, who arrived in Venezuela in 1949 with her husband Simon Lebovic, according to the Venezuelan Red Cross records. These records list the entire Goldberger family in Venezuela following the release of Aranka Goldberger from the Czech jail. The above document was sent to a German institution that wanted to honor Fanny Thoman by hanging a plaque in her honor in the villa located at Berlin–Dahlen, Kesserstrasse 21, Berlin, Germany. In 1940 the Gestapo forced her to move to Berlin–Charlottenburg, Berliner Strasse 97, Brelin. In October 1943 she was sent to the Ravensbruck concentration camp with her niece Lenke Goldberger. Fanny Thoman was murdered at the camp on February 5th, 1945. Apparently, she left all her possessions to her niece, Lenke Goldberger. The Berlin institution wanted permission from a Thoman relative to hang the memorial plaque.

The Goldberger export–import electrical machinery company in Caracas, Venezuela

Armin Goldberger was not involved in the life of the small Jewish community of Caracas. He distanced himself from Jewish life. He devoted himself to a small electrical business that he owned. Armin slowly introduced Toman to life in Venezuela. He began to work in the company and helped expand the business. But his past followed him. Czech refugee groups in the USA started to protest the help that the C.I.A. (Central Intelligence Agency) was extending to Toman. Rumors even circulated that he would reach the USA. These rumors were of course dissipated when Toman did not go there, but headed to South America. The Czech and Russian secret services followed Toman and still hoped to get him back to Prague.

The Czech embassy in Venezuela demanded that the Venezuelan government arrest and detain Toman since he was a fugitive of the law. Interpol had a charge sheet against him which stated that he had committed crimes in Czechoslovakia and must return to Prague to face the charges. The Venezuelan justice minister ordered the arrest of Toman and initiated a hearing of deportation. Armin used all his connections to slow down the legal process, but this was an international dispute between two countries, and Goldberger was not in a position to halt proceedings at such a high level of government. Someone was needed to put a great deal of pressure on the government in

Caracas to halt the proceedings. Apparently, Toman provided Armin with an address to call in time of emergency, and this was certainly an emergency for Toman as well as for the American Intelligence Community. The C.I.A. did not want a Russian debriefing of Toman and decided to act. The case was shifted from one court to another. Along the way, some charges were dropped and eventually the entire case was dismissed and Toman was sent home. Needless to say, it was a terrible experience for Toman and he began looking out for himself.

The Czech secret service was furious but there was little they could do. The trial had to go on with one live person. On June 23rd, 1949, the trial of Toman and his associates began. The sessions were closed to the public. The Czech state accused Zdenek Toman of serious crimes, black market operations and contacts with foreign agents. Imre Rosenberg was charged with black market operations and Aranka Rosenberg–Goldberg was also charged with similar charges. Below are the accusations.

A host of witnesses who worked with Toman began to tell all kinds of stories about smuggling operations that supposedly Toman initiated. He used Czech secret agents to export jewelry and import hard currency. He and his brother–in–law dealt in foreign currency. The profits were huge and implications were made that some of the money went to the Communist party coffers as well as to officials that received gifts and benefits. Of course, Toman made a great deal of money. He was also charged with dealing with foreign agents and divulging state secrets. He was even accused of working with the Gestapo[3]. Of course, none of the party hierarchy was even mentioned at the trial. The witnesses rambled on about deals and combinations as if Toman did nothing but sell and buy goods on the black market. Yet this man handled the repatriation of thousands of people following the war, he ran the state security and the foreign intelligence and was deeply involved in the transportation of Jews across Czechoslovakia. The aim of the trial was to paint Toman as a greedy Jew interested in money and power. He was ready to sell state secrets for money.[4] All these charges fitted the usual Stalinist charges aimed at Jewish communists namely that they were cosmopolitan elements without roots. These charges would be repeated constantly in different variations against Jewish communists in Eastern Europe[5].

The verdict was announced. Zdenek Toman/Goldberger was found guilty of all charges and condemned to death in absentia and loss of all possessions in favor of the state. Imre Rosenberg was found guilty of all charges and, in absentia, condemned to hard labor for life and loss of all property. Aranka Goldberger–Rosenberg was found guilty as charged and received 15 years of hard labor. The child Ivan Toman was placed in the custody of the state at the state shelter of Stvanice in Prague. The sentences were immediately carried out; Aranka Goldberger–Rosenberg was immediately taken to jail while the infant, Ivan Toman remained at the state shelter. Aranka's requests to see her nephew were rejected. She could not even obtain the shelter's address. The Czech secret services began to move the child from place to place until he disappeared.

Or I 63%/49

41

R o z s u d e k .

v J m é n e m r e p u b l i k y .

Státní soud v Praze, odd XIV., uznal po hlavním přeličení provedeném dne 23.6.1949 právem:

Obžalovaní:

1./Dr Zdeněk T o m a n ./Zoltán Goldberger/, nar.2.3.1909 v Sobrancích, ryt. ministerský rada, naposledy bytem v Praze XVIII, Pavlovni 6, t.č. neznámého pobytu v cizině,

2./Dr Jindřich R o s e n b e r g. nar.27.3.1913 v Novém Městě nad Váhom, soukromník, naposledy bytem v Praze XVI, Tichá 1, t.č. neznámého pobytu v cizině,

3./Amálie R o s e n b e r g o v á, roz. Goldberg ová, č. .8.4.191? v Sobrancích, v domácnosti, poslední bytem v Praze XVI, Tichá 1, t.č. v řádné vyšetřovací vazbě státního soudu v Praze

I./ j s o u v i n n i, že

1./Dr Zdeněk Toman, uprchnuv illegálně dne 18.7.1948 do nepřátelské ciziny se zvlášť významní informací, jichž nabyl jako vedoucí úředník zpravodajské služby, sdělil tyto s hlediska obrany státu velmi důležité infor: mace orgánům zpravodajské služby cizí moci a spojil se státu, kteří sledují

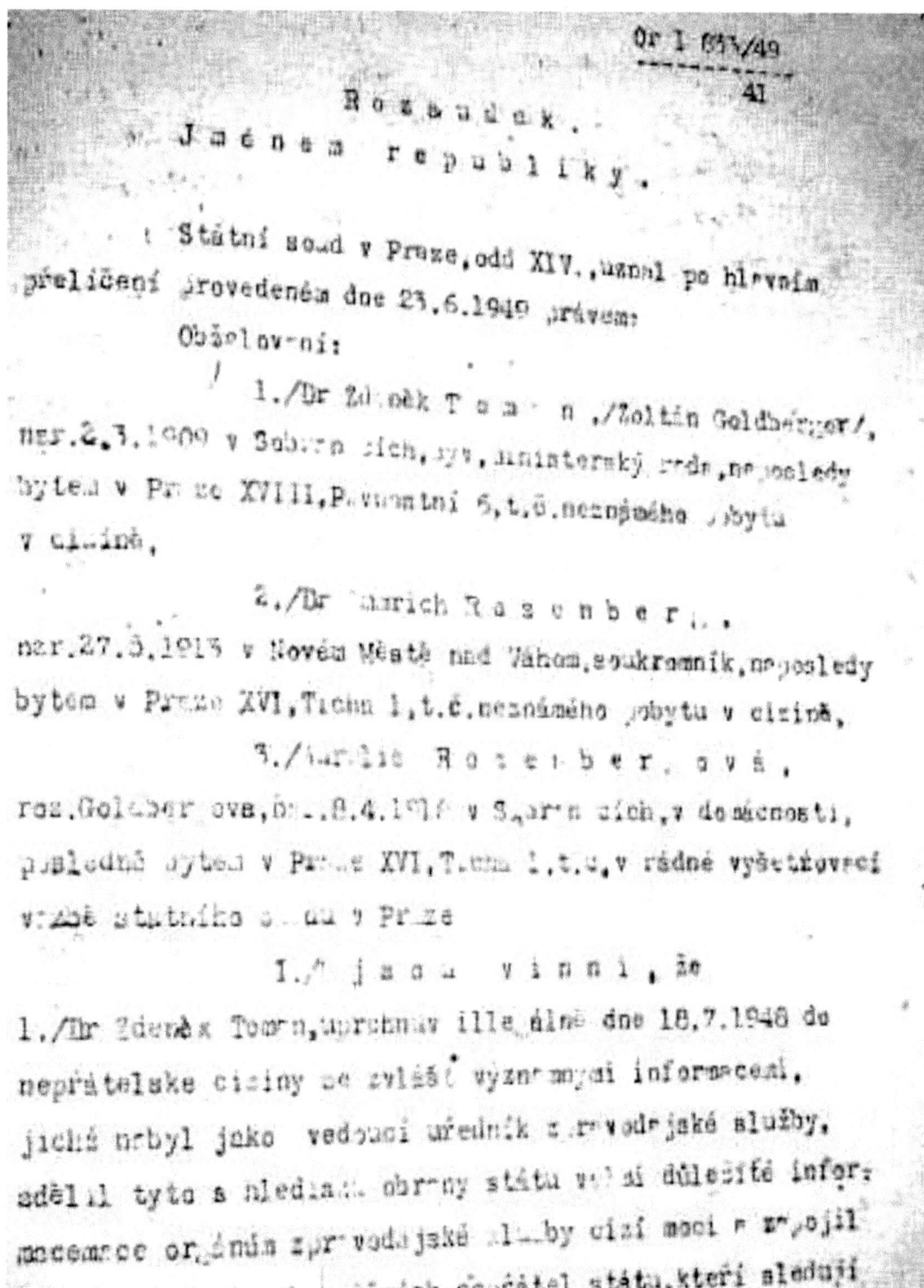

Charge sheet of the accused

Stalin was displeased with the abysmal performance of the trial in Prague that involved a lonely Jewish woman survivor that never held a high government post. He wanted action. The cold war increased in intensity and he insisted on using an iron hand in his Soviet Empire. Already the Soviet press was attacking Jews as being rootless and cosmopolitan. The campaign would reach its crescendo with the arrest of the Jewish doctors who supposedly were plotting to poison Stalin. Already in May of 1949, a team of Soviet NKVD security agents went to Hungary to weed out so–called dissidents within the Hungarian Communist party. In May 1949, Laszlo Rajk, former interior minister and present minister of foreign affairs was arrested for being an agent of Tito and Imperialism. The trial began September 16th and finished on September 24th, 1948. All accused confessed to all the accusations. Laszlo Rajk was condemned to death with two other important Communist leaders. The Rajk series of trials resulted in the death of 15 Communist Hungarian leaders and the imprisonment of 78 Communist leaders. The state terror machine sprang into action. All Jewish and Zionist associations were disbanded in Poland. The Joint organization was ordered to close its operations in Poland[6]. In January 1950, the Joint office in Czechoslovakia was ordered to close its doors[7]. Jewish organizations were disbanded. Czech–Israeli bilateral connections were closing down. Even the military agreements were being finalized and completed. Aranka appealed her verdict to the Czech Supreme Court on April 3rd 1950 as being too harsh. The appeal was rejected[8]. Slansky decided to regain Soviet sympathy following the Toman episode and asked Stalin for help in weeding out dissidents in Czechoslovakia. Stalin soon sent him the Soviet NKVD specialists that handled the Laszlo Rajk case in Hungary. The latter began to investigate the entire Czech government. At first they arrested two Israeli citizens who were members of a left–wing party in Israel that supported the Soviet Union. Both, Mordechai Oren and Szymon Orenstein disappeared without a trace. Months passed and finally a charge sheet appeared against Oren as being a Trotskyite–Titoist–Zionist spy connected to American imperialism. He was brought to trial and confessed to all charges. He was extremely well coached in his lines. He was condemned to 15 years in prison and his friend Orenstein received life. Now the real trial began; Slansky was arrested and with him 13 members of the government and the party. They were all accused of being Titoists, Zionists and connected with imperialist agents. Most of the Czech Communists leaders on trial were Jews. They all confessed to their crimes in open show trials. Eleven were condemned to death, amongst them the Deputy Minister of Defense Bedrich Reicin formerly Reinzinger. Bedrich was an old Bolshevik who worked for the party prior to World War II. The Gestapo arrested him and then released him. He then managed to flee to Russia and returned with the Czech army to Czechoslovakia. He knew Toman from before the war. Reicin was very influential in the military establishment of the country and helped to speed up the purchase of weapons by the Haganah and later by the State of Israel.

Czechoslovakia had a large military industry as well as huge stocks of light and heavy weapons that the German army had left in the country at the end of the war. The Haganah tried to purchase weapons for the expected battles in Palestine but it was not very successful. One of the problems was that most sellers wanted hard cash and instant delivery. The Haganah could not purchase weapons and send them to Palestine in one shipment; the weapons had to be smuggled in small quantities to the country: a long, tedious and costly process. Furthermore, the British secret services made sure that the arms dealers were forewarned not to sell weapons to the Jews. The Haganah agent in Czechoslovakia was Felix Doron or Felix Michael who decided to approach Toman via Jacobson. Toman could issue such permits being the deputy Interior Minister. He also probably consulted Reicin on the feelings within the Defense Ministry regarding the sale of weapons to "Haganah" in Palestine. Apparently the answer was in the affirmative. Toman then called on Doron who was a native Czech speaker and studied at the Charles University. Doron was familiar with many students that presently held high positions in the government and may have even known Toman in his student days. Toman presented the request to purchase weapons by the "Haganah" to a meeting that included Gottwald, Nosek, General Ludwig Svoboda, Minister of Defense and Toman himself[9]. Masaryk was also consulted on the deal. Moshe Sneh, member of the Jewish Agency was sent to Czechoslovakia by Ben Gurion[10], head of the Jewish Agency for Palestine. He met Gottwald and stressed the need for the weapons and the certainty of payment. The Czechs approved the deal and orders were issued to permit the Haganah to purchase weapons. The technical arrangements were hastily processed with the assistance of Bedrich Reicin, assistant to the Czech Defense Minister[11]. Ehud Avriel in his book "Open the Gates" gives us a glimpse of the speed in which arms transactions took place[12]. Avriel met an agent named Robert Adam in Paris who was well connected with the Czech arms industry and both flew to Prague where arms deals were signed[13]. The first weapons deal was signed on January 10th 1948 and most of the weapons of this purchase reached Palestine on April 23rd 1948[14]. The first purchase would be followed by other arms purchases. This trade would expand and include fighter planes, the training of fighter pilots and the establishment of an Israeli air base at the Zatec airfield next to the East German border. This base would operate for several months: May – August 1948. Big American transport planes would fly weapons and ammunition from Zatec airfield to Tel Aviv and return empty[15]. The weapons would be crucial in the fight for Israel's survival. These weapon transactions would continue for some time to come while the initiators, Toman was already under house arrest, and Reicin would be arrested in 1952 and condemned to death. The weapon issue was never mentioned at Toman's trial.

Footnotes

1. Aranka's testimony at her trial in Prague.
2. Aranka's police file in Prague.
3. Czech police records dealing with the trial.
4. See trial records in Czech
5. Rudolf Slansky would be accused of similar charges in 1952 and would be condemned to death.
6. Szulc, Alliance pp.200–201
7. Ibid., p. 201
8. See the Czech document.
9. Szulc, Alliance p.156
10. Yehuda Bauer. Out of the Ashes, p.132.
11. He was born to a poor Jewish family by the name of Reinzinger. He joined the Communist party in the thirties and in WWII served with the Czechoslovak Army under the command of Svoboda. Reicin also headed counter military intelligence.
12. Ehud Avriel, Open the Gates p.334.
13. Ibid p.334
14. A small amount of rifles and ammunition arrived by plane on April 3rd 1948. The big shipment arrived on April 23rd 1948 aboard the ship "*Norafrom*" from Yugoslavia. The shipment comprised 10,000 rifles, a number of machine guns and a large amount of ammunition. By October 1948, Czechoslovakia had sold 46751 rifles, 6142 machine guns of various types, 80 million rounds of ammunition and some fighter planes to Israel.
15. Most of the fliers were Jewish WWII war pilots and most of the planes were smuggled out of the USA.

Chapter XII
Toman the Jewish Benefactor

The Goldbergers sent letters and money to Aranka in jail. They tried to make her life more pleasant, which was not easy in this period of Stalinist terror in Czechoslovakia. Toman feels especially guilty since he left his sister by herself in a Czech prison. True but there was little he could do. He writes long letters and tries to cheer her up. Occasionally, she gets a letter from her husband who left England and arrived penniless in Canada, where he started doing odd jobs to keep going, and then started to deal in real estate. He was naturalized in Canada in 1954, and later joined the academic world. He wrote less and less to Aranka since he had met Truda Osterman a psychologist. They started dating. Rosenberg decided to divorce Aranka and sent divorce papers to her in prison. We can imagine the severe psychological blow to Aranka, but she survived. Rosenberg married Truda. At first they lived in Israel and then returned to Canada where he worked with the Canadian government on many projects. He died in 1986.

Aranka continued trying to locate her nephew but all attempts failed. She wrote to the Czech Red Cross, but received no reply. Similar appeals were made by Lenka and Toman without results. Toman entered the business world and became very successful. All attempts to communicate with the state shelter where Ivan Toman was supposedly residing were answered with a laconic reply that he no longer lived there. The boy seemed to be beyond reach.

Toman left his brother's residence and rented a place of his own in town. The landlady was Maria Monardi, who was of Italian extraction. Slowly, the tenant–owner relationship turned more intimate. Mrs. Monardi was a divorced woman with three daughters from a previous marriage. They all lived in the Monardi apartment. Monardi soon joined Toman on his business trips.

The Goldberger brothers expanded the business. Toman attended fairs and bought and sold machinery. The "Gexim" company expanded and hired more people. They even began to do business with the USA, according to the FBI (Federal Bureau of Investigation) that had to approve Toman's entry requests to visit the USA on business. Toman even had a representative in New York named Joseph Barrocas who resided in Brooklyn, New York.

The latter party handled all the negotiations in the USA for the Goldberger brothers. On occasion Toman visited the USA to finalize purchases of machinery that was then shipped to Venezuela. The FBI had an extensive record of Toman's past, and whenever he was in the USA, he was always followed by FBI agents.

Excerpt from FBI file regarding Toman's visit to the USA

Toman began to travel to Europe and approached many organizations: the International Red Cross, the Czech Red Cross and many humanitarian associations to help locate his son. He even contacted many Czech officials and private lawyers to help locate the boy but all efforts failed. Of course, Toman did not venture to cross the border to Czechoslovakia where his sentence was still in effect, so he did the next best thing – he went to Vienna, from where he directed his fruitless efforts. Even his sister, Aranka Goldberger, who was released from jail in 1961, failed to locate the boy. She searched and searched, but in vain. With the end of her probation period, Aranka left Czechoslovakia and joined her brothers and sister in Venezuela. Toman continued to visit Europe; he also visited the West Coast, notably California. He liked the state, especially the Santa Barbara area. He applied for a visa to stay in the USA for a longer period, but was turned down.[1] Below is the document that shows his rejection. Toman appealed the decision and used his contacts. He was finally permitted to stay for some time in the USA as the document indicates.

Toman continued his search for his son by all means. The Czech secret police frequently released disinformation leaks about the boy but never told the exact story as to what happened to the child. A fake Ivan Toman was once presented to Aranka and her sister Lenka but they did not recognize him as Ivan Toman. Czech ministers came and went and still no trace of Ivan Toman. Then there was a rumor that Ivan Toman was given for adoption to a family, when a convenient accident occurred and the boy was injured and then died. Of course, the family was never notified of his adoption or of his death. The Czech secret police played a cruel game with the poor child, even his burial place was not revealed to the family. Letters and requests were formulated and answered.

Interdepartmental memos were sent and answered. Entire files were established but no trace was found of Ivan Toman. The secret services kept the entire story under wraps for years. Eventually, most of the parties involved in the story retired or left their place of work. New people came that did not know the story and did not care to look for problems. The Ivan Toman enigma remained unsolved.

Toman continued to travel to Europe and bought a great deal of art works in Italy that he shipped back home to Venezuela. His sister Aranka met and married a man named Resnick. They opened a business similar to that of Toman but on a much smaller scale. Then Toman decided to make a lengthy visit to the USA. He requested permission for a visa and was denied

He appealed the decision and was granted the visa. The FBI of course followed him everywhere and reported every move that he made as the report indicates.

Aranka visited Czechoslovakia in 1973 and decided to ask the court for her rehabilitation of all the charges and restoration of her rights as a citizen. Her request was granted. She also petitioned the High Court for the rehabilitation of her brother Zdenek Toman originally Zdenek Goldberger who was condemned to death on June 23, 1949. The court rejected the appeal on behalf of Toman on the grounds that he left Czechoslovakia without legal permission. Toman would eventually receive a partial pardon but he never trusted the Czech authorities and never again set foot on Czechoslovakian soil. The Czech judicial officials continued to work until they retired.

Toman began to spend more time on the West Coast, Israel, and Europe. He limited himself to Vienna where he continued to contact people to locate his son's whereabouts.[2] He became active in the Jewish community of California, namely in the Bnei Brith Organization. He also contributed financially to the American political parties. He began to socialize. He married Maria and they visited Europe and Israel where, in 1977 he presented three classical paintings to the Tel Aviv Museum. The first painting is attributed to Bernardo Bellotto of the 17th century, pupil and nephew of the great Italian painter Canaletto. Bellotto painted urban landscapes namely the city of Dresden, Germany. Toman presented the "View of Dresden" to the Museum. He also donated two paintings depicting Venice by Luca Calavaris, who lived and died in Venice in the 18th century[3]. He was mostly known for his paintings of Venetian scenes. The presentation of the paintings was followed by a large luncheon in honor of the Sobrance Jewish survivors in Israel. According to Anna, a native of Sobrance, she and others received invitations to attend the banquet, fully paid by Toman.

Toman became very active in the Bnei Brith organization on the West Coast. He contributed financially to the organization and supported it. He also donated contributions to various philanthropic organizations.

UNITED STATES DEPARTMENT OF JUSTICE
Immigration and Naturalization Service
Miami, Florida

March 29, 1967

File: A13 139 035

In re: Zoltan TOMAN Toman, aka Zoltan Goldberger

APPLICATION: Temporary admission to the United States pursuant to
section 212(d)(3)(A) of the Immigration and Nationality
Act, despite inadmissibility under section 212(a)(28)
of the Act.

The applicant, a citizen and resident of Venezuela, born March 2, 1909,
at Sobrance, Czechoslovakia, has been found by the Department of State
to be ineligible to receive a visa because of his past membership in
the Communist Party of Czechoslovakia. He is the owner of General Export Import, C. A., a machinery and tool firm in Caracas, Venezuela,
which conducts a large volume of business each year with the United
States. He wishes to enter the United States by air at New York, New
York, on or before June 15, 1967, for the purpose of conducting business for his company, having a medical examination and visiting his
daughter who is married to a United States citizen. At various times
during the next six months he plans to visit New York, New York, and
Kansas City, Missouri.

Temporary admission of the applicant has been previously authorized on
several occasions, the last on June 22, 1966, and there is no indication that he violated any of the terms of those admissions. The responsible consular officer and the Embassy at Caracas recommend that admission be authorized in the facilitation of trade and business. Upon careful consideration of the information relating to the applicant and the
recommendation of the Department of State reflecting the benefits which
will accrue to the United States by virtue of the temporary admission,
it is concluded that the recommendation should be approved.

IT IS ORDERED that the application be granted, subject to revocation at
any time, valid for one entry on or before June 15, 1967, at New York,
New York, for a period of four weeks, and for multiple additional en-
tries prior to September 29, 1967, for the above indicated purposes.

NOT RECORDED

APR 10 1967

DISTRICT DIRECTOR

The FBI document authorizing Toman's stay in the USA for a period of time

The Bnai Brith organization in California decided to recognize his activities by organizing a luncheon in his honor. The guest speaker at the luncheon was Congressman Tom Lantos, the only Shoah survivor to be elected to the United States Congress. Many Shoah survivors from Czechoslovakia were invited to the luncheon. Toman continued with his philanthropic activities in the USA and especially in Israel where he concentrated on cultural and educational projects. He loved the State of Israel where he saw all the people that he helped to cross Czechoslovakia on their way to Palestine. He saw them as they were then and he saw them now. What a change from humble people to proud citizens of their own country. He traveled extensively throughout the country and was amazed at the development of Israel. In Israel he met his old friend Jacobson who introduced him to leading political figures in the country. He also met the Mossad and Brichah people that he had heard so much about. Indeed these were happy moments for Toman, seeing what these people achieved and the great help that he extended to make this possible.

The Anti-Defamation League

of B'nai B'rith

Pacific Southwest Region

Invites You To A Luncheon

With

Congressman Tom Lantos   Dr. Zoltan Toman

dedicated to translating democratic ideals into a way of life for all Americans in our life time

The AntiDefamation League of B'nai B'rith
Pacific Southwest Region
Cordially Requests the Pleasure of Your Company
at its Spring Meeting
featuring the

Torch of Liberty Award
to
Dr. Zoltan Toman

Guest Speaker
the Honorable Tom Lantos

Sunday, May 23, 1982
Ballroom
Beverly Wilshire Hotel
Beverly Hills, California

11:30 A.M. - Registration   Couvert $20.00
12:00 Noon - Luncheon   Per Person
2:30 P.M. - Adjournment

No Solicitation of Funds

Toman is presented with the award of the Bnei Brith organization in the USA for his contribution to the American Jewish community. Copy graciously donated by Anna Neufeld née Keller

Toman devoted himself to the educational needs of Israel, especially in the South that was populated to a great extent by immigrants. A great favorite institution of his was the Ben–Gurion University of the Negev in Beersheba, in the desert. He visited the place and donated large sums of money to help the university provide an education to as many youngsters as possible. When he spoke at the university, he stressed the need for education in order to survive in the modern world. He frequently visited, and devoted himself to the expansion of the learning facility.

The Pesla Toman Gutman building donated in 1987 was in honor of Toman's first wife who died under suspicious circumstances that as yet, have never been revealed

Dedication of the Maria and Zoltan Toman endowment fund for academic excellence. Seated on the left is Zoltan Toman, then the master of ceremonies. Standing and welcoming the guest is Avishay Braverman President of Ben–Gurion University and later Minister of Minorities in the Israeli government.

Here is a list of gifts from the Toman family to the Ben–Gurion University in Beersheba:

Toman Family Department of Life Sciences Building
Zoltan Toman Equipment Endowment Fund
Zoltan Toman Library Endowment Fund
Maria and Zoltan Toman Endowment Fund for Academic Excellence
Zoltan Toman Medical Research Fund
Zoltan Toman General Research Endowment Fund
The Pesla Toman Gutman building donated in 1987
The University in turn bestowed the greatest honors on Zoltan Toman for his devotion, contribution and work on behalf of the university. In 1982, he was awarded an honorary degree of Doctor of Philosophy by the University at a formal ceremony.

Dr. Zoltan Toman accepts honorary degree from Ben Gurion University

The Ben Gurion University presented the Tomans with their highest award namely the "Lifetime Achievement Award" for their extensive services on behalf of the university. Toman and his wife Maria named Ben–Gurion University as a benefactor in their will.

The Tomans slowly gave up hope of ever finding Ivan Toman. They invested a great deal of energy, money and time without results. All the appeals to the various international and local Czech humanitarian organizations proved fruitless. The personal intervention of Aranka and Lenka Goldberger were to no avail. Zoltan Toman never returned to Czechoslovakia. We do not know whether fear or old age prevented him from stepping on to Czech soil. The Toman case did not die, it kept reappearing from time to time and embarrassed the Czech government and the judicial system. Eventually, in the early 1990s the Czech government decided to investigate the Toman case and many other similar cases.

Dr. Zoltan and Maria Toman being presented with the Lifetime Achievement Award at Ben Gurion University

Footnotes

1. Consular letter to that effect
2. Ibid. p.7
3. Information graciously provided by the Tel Aviv Museum.

Chapter XIII
Ivan Toman

**Tombstone of Michael Rohan (born Nov. 2, 1947, died March 7, 1961).
Next to him is buried Ludmila Rohan, his adopted mother
(born Feb. 24,1907, died Sept. 26,1988)**

The image above pictures the tombstone of Michael Rohan, born November 2, 1947 and died March 7, 1961. He was adopted by the childless couple, Jiri and Ludmila Rohan. Rohan worked for the Czech secret service. When he was a teenager, the child was involved in an accident and died. Many years later, the Czech secret service insisted that Michael Rohan was actually Ivan Toman. Zdenek Toman did not buy the story.

With the changing of the political climate in Europe, particularly in Czechoslovakia, the post–Communist Czech governments faced a great deal of pressure from various humanitarian groups as to the whereabouts of Ivan

Toman. The government would not answer since it did not know the details of the case. The Czech secret service kept releasing uninformative statements that led nowhere. The Czech government decided to create an office of investigation to investigate unsolved crimes that were committed during the Communist regime. The office consisted of top police investigators and researchers. They worked, researched and examined all the relevant offices and reports on the cases. They even interviewed people, including Aranka Toman–Resnik and Zdenek Toman in California. A former political prisoner named Jozef Bacon who knew Aranka was sent to California to interview her and her brother Zdenek. Still no clues or traces were found that shed light on Ivan's disappearance. Months and years passed and still no clue. It is evident that some of the investigators did not want to find clues since they or their friends were deeply involved in the various cover–up stories. Eventually, the Czech police decided to solve the case.

The investigators returned to the original arrest warrants, investigations and court proceedings. The record of the verdict states that Zoltan Toman/ Goldberger was condemned in absentia to death and all of his possessions were to be turned over to the government. His possessions were his apartment in Prague and a bank deposit book containing 50,341.10 Czech korunas.[1] Toman's wife, Pesla, also had a bank book with 249,890.90 Czech korunas. The investigators began to search the bank records and luck was with them. They found the Toman account books but they were closed. Zdenek Toman/ Goldberger's account was closed on February 18, 1949, prior to his trial that took place on June 23, 1949. The man who closed the account was Captain Alois Male of the Czech security police. The act was highly illegal if not criminal. Toman was still legally an innocent man and nobody had the right to close his account. Apparently, higher officials than the captain ordered the bank to close the account. Pesla Toman's account was closed by Alois Male of the Czech security police on March 16, 1950. This closure was a plain common robbery since Pesla Toman had not been charged with any crime. The money was hers or her descendants'. Male went one step further and established a trust fund in the amount of 259,480 Czech korunas[2] for Ivan Toman whose foster father was Prague resident Jiri Rohan.

Jiri Rohan was a regular driver for the security police. He was married to Ludmila and they had no children. The Rohan family wanted a child and Jiri kept asking the officers for a child. One day, the Rohans were presented with a baby. They were told that he was found abandoned in the town of Jihlava, quite a distance from the city of Prague. Attached to the baby was a note stating that his name was Michael and 10,000 Czech korunas.[3] The couple adopted Michael and gave him their last name, Rohan. Michael was registered as Michael Rohan born on November 2nd, 1947. No legitimate birth certificate was ever presented as to the authenticity of the child. Until today, the names of the father and mother of the child are not known. The cities of Prague and Jihlava had no listing of an unwanted child on this particular day. Yet a baby was presented to the Rohans by the security police. The baby was even provided with a nice trust fund. Apparently a few Czech security agents were involved in these bizarre machinations. They had the approval and protection of the Interior Minister, Vaclav Nosek.

Ivan Toman remained at the state shelter for a short time and then he was moved from place to place by security officers. Even the state shelter did not know where the child wound up. All inquiries as to the whereabouts of the child were ignored or sent to the wrong address. Aranka tried to get in touch with the shelter from her prison in Prague but failed to establish contact. Even the Czech Red Cross tried to intervene but to no avail.

Years later, an accident occurred and Michael Rohan was seriously injured and rushed to a military hospital in Prague where he was unconscious for about 50 days and died on March 7, 1961, under the name of Michael Rohan.[4] He was 14 years of age. He never knew his original name, his family or his origin. He was cremated and the urn containing his ashes was buried at plot number 288 at the Motol Crematoria. Years later, his adoptive mother was buried next to him. The Czech investigators never solved the mysterious disappearance of Ivan Toman. They slowly started to spread the idea that Michael Rohan and Ivan Toman were one and the same person. With time and persistence many people accepted the story. Czech officials even visited the Goldberger sisters and presented them with their findings. These findings were also shown to Zdenek Toman but he was doubtful. The sisters went to Czechoslovakia on several occasions and visited the grave of their supposed nephew but not Toman. As a matter of fact, the last codicil of his will, probated on June 3, 1998, set aside $10,000 for Ivan Toman, a clear indication that he was doubtful about the entire Czech story about his son. No real tests were ever performed to ascertain whose ashes were buried at the cemetery next to Ludmila Rohan. Toman was familiar with the methods of the Czech secret police and he did not trust them. Ivan was not the only missing child in Czechoslovakia.[5]

With advancing age, Zdenek Toman reduced his social activities and trips. He spent more time in his sumptuous home in California surrounded by many beautiful art works that he had acquired in Europe, according to Avishay Braverman, President of Ben–Gurion University.[6]

Toman drew up a will on December 23, 1991 in which he left everything to his wife Maria M. Toman and to her three daughters, Marina Mayers, Maura Lundi and Patricia Braukman and their children. He also mentioned in the will his son Ivan Toman whose whereabouts in Czechoslovakia were unknown. The document is quite extensive and deals with Toman's assets in the United States. No mention was made of assets in Venezuela if they existed nor is the Goldberger family mentioned in the document. This seems a bit strange since Toman was close to his sister Aranka. Toman sent her checks while she was in prison in Czechoslovakia and took great interest in her well–being. Aranka helped Pesla Toman and her son Ivan while Zdenek Toman was away at the so-called health farm and Toman sent a car to bring Aranka to Prague right after the war. These two siblings became very close and Toman did everything in his power to help Aranka.

But suddenly, relations among the Goldbergers cooled. Toman's new family started to distance itself from the rest of the Goldbergers. As a matter of fact, Cecille Goldberger, niece of Toman, stated in a letter that the Goldbergers had little contact with the Toman family.[7] This could explain why the Goldberger family is not mentioned in Zdenek Toman's will. Nor were there any bequests made to Jewish or non–Jewish social or welfare agencies. This is strange indeed for a family that donated so much charity. Everything was left to the Toman family.

Maria Toman and her daughters even contested a document that Zdenek Toman signed with Ben–Gurion University in which he pledged to contribute $5 million for the construction of a new learning facility at the campus of the institution in Beersheba. Payments were supposed to start with the beginning of the construction. However Toman died before construction began. When the university began construction, it notified Toman. The latter's estate did not reply. The university hired lawyers who took the case to court where the family was forced to appear and explain the reason for non–payment of the promissory note. The case was settled out of court.

`Zdenek Toman died on December 20, 1997, in the resort area of Cabo in Mexico. Toman's will was probated June 3, 1998. His body was removed from the Mexican cemetery on June 24, 1998, and he was reburied in Caracas, Venezuela. His sister Aranka died on April 21, 1999, and Lenka Goldberger followed. Maria M. Toman died in 2003 and was buried in Santa Barbara, California. She left her belongings to her three daughters. The descendants of Armin Goldberger reside in Venezuela and in the United States.

Asher Zelig Goldberger or Zdenek Toman saved thousands of Jewish Shoah survivors by enabling them to cross Czechoslovakia and escape the areas of Eastern Europe infested with anti–Semitism. Jews, especially in Poland, felt insecure and began to leave. They headed mostly to the Czech border posts, which they crossed, and where they received temporary shelter. The American Joint Distribution Committee provided the money and the Brichah provided the guides to move these refugees to Germany, Austria and Italy where they took up residence in the D.P. camps. Their number was staggering and reached about 250,000 by the end of 1947. Britain and the United States pressured Czechoslovakia to close its borders but Toman kept them open. The large refugee population in the camps provided the manpower that challenged the British navy and eventually forced Britain to abandon Palestine. Most of the Jewish refugees went to Israel and started a new life. Toman, on his visits to Israel, was pleased to meet the people he had helped.

Asher Zelig Goldberger wrote a beautiful chapter in Jewish history.

May he rest in peace.

Zdenek Goldberger Toman resting peacefully in Venezuela

Footnotes

1. The exchange rate was about $1=50 Czech crowns
2. http/www.vasevec.cz/blg/ctvrty–musketyt–leta–pane–styricateo=osmeho–6. p.8
3. Czech police file
4. http/www.vasevec.cz/blg/ctvrty–musketyt–leta–pane–styricateo=osmeho–6. p.8
5. Many children of so–called politically unreliable parents were given up for adoption without leaving any traces, as reported by Ms. Uzlova in an interview in the Globes newspaper. She herself has never been able to find her mother or sister.
6. Larry Price interview with Avishay Braverman.
7. Letter received from Cecille Goldberger.

Appendix: Partial List of Sobrance Jews

*Sources:
YV - Yad Vashem, Jerusalem P - Private research
Note: All those listed here, unless otherwise noted, were killed in the Holocaust

Last name	First name	Birth date	Gender	Source*	Remarks
ACKERMAN	Kalman	1922	M	YV	
ADLER	Andi		M	YV	
AMSTER	Julia	1939	F	YV	
AMSTER	Gizelle	1914	F	YV	
AMSTER	Julia		F	YV	
AMSTER	Julika	1938	F	YV	
AMSTER	Henrik	1908	M	YV	
BALSAM	Max	27/07/1922	M	YV	
BALSAM	Roza	1893	F	YV	
BALSAM	David	8/03/1920	M	YV	
BAMBERGER	Jolana	1/11/1919	F	YV	
BERGER	Jakob	1892	M	YV	
BERGER	Dwora	1922	F	YV	
BERKOVIC	Hannah		F	YV	
BERKOVIC	Tzipora		F	YV	
BERKOVIC	Rachel		F	YV	
BERKOVIC	Etel	1916	F	YV	
BERKOVIC	Eliezar	1931	M	YV	
BERKOVIC	Feige	1929	F	YV	
BERKOVIC	Meir	1927	M	YV	
BERKOVIC	Henia	1934	F	YV	
BERKOVIC	Berl		M	YV	
BERKOVICCZ	Dov		M	YV	
BERKOVICCZ	Meir		M	YV	
BERKOVICZ	Malka	1897	F	YV	
BERKOVITCH	Regina	11/09/1906	F	YV	
BERKOVITZ	Samuel	1893	M	YV	
BERKOVIZ	Shmuel	25/12/1893	M	YV	
BIRENBAUM	Rezel	1897	F	YV	
BISTRICER	Itzhak		M	YV	
BISTRICER	Tzvi		M	YV	
BISTRICER	Tova		F	YV	
BOMBERGER	Yolana	1/11/1919	F	YV	
BREUER	Alice	28/01/1929	F	YV	
BREUER	Willam	25/12/1900	M	YV	
BREUER	Irene	1/05/1907	F	YV	
CIN	Szajndel	1870	F	YV	
DAVIDOVITS	Aaron	1917	M	YV	

DEUTSCH	Shaul	1889	M	YV	
DEUTSCH	Zalman	1909	M	YV	
EICHLER	Shaya		M	YV	
ELOVIC	Mina	9/3/1889	F	YV	
ELOVICS	Sandor	4/06/1912	M	YV	
ELOVITCH	Max	17/02/1905	M	YV	
EOSNER	Yoosif	1893	M	YV	
FARKASH	Yolanda	1905	M	YV	
FARKASH	Mikshe	1900	M	YV	
FEIGENBAUM	I		M	YV	
FEUREISEN	Dora	1875	F	YV	
FEURSTEIN	Josef	9/1885	M	YV	
FISHEROVA	Jolana	1909	F	YV	
FLEISCHER	Gizelle	6/03/1912	F	YV	
FRANKEL	Rachel	1898	F	YV	
FRANTISKA	Kamiolova	18/2/1875	F	YV	
FRIED	Mojsze	24/02/1905	M	YV	
FRIED	Etil		F	YV	
FRIED	Leah		F	YV	
FRIED	Pepi		F	YV	
FRIED	Roza	1887	F	YV	
FRIED	Golda		F	YV	
FRIED	Jentl		F	YV	
FRIED	Moshe	1884	M	YV	
FRIED	Genia		F	YV	
FRIEDMAN	Lujza	14/3/1884	f	YV	
FRIEDMAN	Irena	1906	F	YV	
FRIEDMAN	Hercko	1897	M	YV	
FRIEDMAN	Lanke	1883	F	YV	
FRIEDMAN	Abraham	1925	M	YV	
FRIEDMAN	Lenka	1884	F	YV	
FRIEDMANN	Reizl	1904	F	YV	
FRIEDMANN	Moshe		M	YV	
FRIEDMANN	Albert	1/06/1925	M	YV	
FRIEDMANN	Emil		M	YV	
GEB	Yehudit		F	YV	
GEB	Gizelle		F	YV	
GELB	Meir		M	YV	
GELB	Jolan	1914	M	YV	
GELB	Tova	1913	F	YV	
GLANC	Mordechai	1908	M	YV	
GOLDBERG	David		M	P	
GOLDBERG	Rosalia		F	P	Husband - David
GOLDBERG	Armin		M	P	Parents - David & Rosalia
GOLDBERG	Baruch		M	P	Parents - David & Rosalia
GOLDBERG	Ella		F	P	Maiden name BRAUNFELD. Husband - Baruch
GOLDBERG	Esther	1941	F	P	Parents -

					Baruch & Ella
GOLDBERG	Asher	2/03/1909	M	P	Suvived
GOLDBERG	Pesla	25/12/1912	F	P	Maiden name GUTMAN. Survived.
GOLDBERG	Bella		F	P	
GOLDBERG	Clara		F	P	
GOLDBERG	Lemke	20/01/1917	F	P	Survived
GOLDBERG	Aranka	8/04/1918	F	P	Survived
GOLDBERGER	Ella	1914	F	P	
GOLDBERGER	Mordechai		M	P	
GOLDBERGER	Frimet		F	P	
GREENBERGER	Moshe		M	YV	
GREENBERGER	Aliza		F	YV	
GREENBERGER	Hannah		M	YV	
GREENBERGER	Jakob		F	YV	
GREENFELD	Berta	1874	F	YV	
GRINFELD	Feige	1912	F	YV	
GRINFELLD	Yehudit		F	YV	
GRINSTEIN	Samuel	1890	M	YV	
GROSSMAN	Chaim		M	YV	
GROSSMAN	Esther	1904	F	YV	
GROSSMAN	Jolana	1909	F	YV	
GROSSMAN	Bluma		F	YV	
GRUENFELD	David	1900	M	YV	
GRUENFELD	Ilana		F	YV	
GRUENFELD	Oilana	18/02/1914	F	YV	
GRUENFELD	Yecheskel	1872	M	YV	
GRUENFELD	Leopold	1886	M	YV	
GRUENSTEIN	Shuel		M	YV	
GRUMBERGER	Anna	1888	F	YV	
GRUMBERGER	Rozsi	1925	F	YV	
GRUMVALD	Ephraim	1887	M	YV	
GRUMVALD	Andre	1907	M	YV	
GRUNBERGER	Sandor	27/10/1919	M	YV	
GRUNBERGER	Roszi	1925	F	YV	
GRUNBERGER	Moric	1934	M	YV	
GRUNBERGER	Aliza	1937	F	YV	
GRUNFELD	Jozsef	29/03/1905	M	YV	
GRUNFELD	Fulop	23/03/1905	M	YV	
GRUNVALD	Sarolda	1885	F	YV	
GRUNWALD	Sandor	21/12/1916	M	YV	
GRUNWALD	Herzog	15/02/1909	M	YV	
GRUNWALD	Charlota	16/1/1882	F	YV	
GUTMAN	Peri		F	YV	
GUTMAN	Hershil		M	YV	
GUTMAN	Heinia		F	YV	
HARSTEIN	Nahum	1915	M	YV	
HENDLER	Iran	1910	M	YV	
HERSHKOVIC	Dr.		M	YV	
HERSHKOVIC	Gisele		F	YV	
HERSHKOVIC	Daniel	1880	M	YV	

HERSHKOVIC	Esther	1885	F	YV	
HERSHKOVIC	Daniel		M	YV	
HERSHKOVIC	Esther		F	YV	Maiden name HENDLER. Husband - Daniel
HERSHKOVIC	Karla		F	YV	Parents - Daniel & Esther
ICKOVIC	Elizabet	1900	F	YV	
ICKOVIC	Ludvig		M	YV	
ILKOVIC	Eugene	1889	M	YV	
ILOVIC	Elizabeth	2/06/1907	F	YV	
ILOVIC	Eva	11/10/1925	F	YV	
ISRAELOVIC	Rachel	1909	F	YV	
IZRAELOVIC	Bella	1906	F	YV	
JACUBOVIC	Margita	30/01/1911	M	YV	
JAKAB	Alfred	16/02/1924	M	YV	
JAKAB	Terezia	1894	F	YV	
JAKUBOVIC	Miksa	18/06/1914	M	YV	
JAKUBOVIC	Paula	6/04/1908	F	YV	
JAKUBOVIC	Ignac	1/3/1876	M	YV	
JAKUBOVIC	Shlomo		M	YV	
JAKUBOVIC	Irmiyahu		M	YV	
JAKUBOVIC	Eisik	16/02/1931	M	YV	
JAKUBOVIC	Anna	1894	F	YV	
JAKUBOVIC	Jakob	1894	M	YV	
JAKUBOVIC	Dvora	1888	F	YV	
JAKUBOVIC	Michal		F	YV	
JAKUBOVICS	David	1891	M	YV	
JAKUBOVICS	Magda	1/05/1921	F	YV	
JAKUBOVICS	Moshe	1886	M	YV	
JAKUBOVICS	Zigmund		M	YV	
JAKUBOVICS	Alexander		M	YV	
JAKUBOVICS	Margita	30/07/1911	F	YV	
JAKUBOVITZ	Anna	20/12/1894	F	YV	
JAKUBOVITZ	Slomo		M	YV	
JAKUBOVITZ	Sgmund		M	YV	
JAKUBOVITZ	Jermias		M	YV	
JAKUBOVITZ	David	1891	M	YV	
JAKUBOVITZ	Miksa		M	YV	
JANKELEVIC	Tova	1916	F	YV	
JUSKOVIC	Arnold	1890	M	YV	
KASTENBAUM	Julius	24/06/1900	F	YV	
KATZ	Aranka	1900	F	YV	
KATZ	Jolan	1/11/1919	F	YV	
KELLER	Leib	1934	M	YV	
KELLER	Baruch	1888	M	YV	
KLEIN	Tibor	1928	M	YV	
KLEIN	Borbela	1900	F	YV	
KLEIN	Roza	1/05/1922	F	YV	
KLEIN	Carolina		F	YV	
KLEIN	Lipot/Yehu	1906	M	YV	
KRAUSZ	Lenka	10/4/1877	F	YV	

KRONOVIC	Miksa	5/08/1931	F	YV	
KRONOVIC	Sari	1902	F	YV	
KRONOVIC	Ignac	1896	M	YV	
KRONOVIC	David	1871	M	YV	
LEBOVITS	Jolan	1908	M	YV	
LEFKOVIC	Szigmond	16/04/1910	M	YV	
LEFKOVIC	Cecilia	11/02/1905	F	YV	
LEFKOVITS	Miksa	1878	F	YV	
LEFKOVITS	Gavriel		M	YV	
LEFKOVITZ	Mikshe		M	YV	
LEIBOVICS	Miksa		M	YV	
LEIBOVITS	Herman		M	YV	
MAJEROVIC	Ida	12/06/1907	F	YV	
MAJEROVIC	Ogen	11/02/1900	M	YV	
MAJEROVITZ	Zwi	1894	M	YV	
MARKOVIC	Ignac	1/3/1876	M	YV	
MILDER	Moric		M	YV	
MILDER	Moric	1893	M	YV	
MILDER	Ladislav		M	YV	
MILDER	Ernest		M	YV	
MILDER	Etelka		F	YV	
MILDER	Laslo		M	YV	
MILDER	Mor		M	YV	
MIRSA	G'orge	4/6/1885	M	YV	
MITTELMAN	Benjamin	1892	M	YV	
MITTELMAN	Jolana	1910	F	YV	
MOSHKOVIC	Hannah	1885	F	YV	
MOSKOVIC	Josef		M	YV	
MOSKOVIC	Giza		F	YV	
MOSKOVIC	Alex		M	YV	
MOSKOVIC	Ernest		M	YV	
MOSKOVIC	Zoltan		M	YV	
MOSKOVIC	Jozsef	2/04/1910	M	YV	
MOSKOVIC	Zlatica	12/10/1909	F	YV	
MOSKOVIC	Simon	22/04/1911	M	YV	
MOSKOVIC	Shmil	1909	M	YV	
MOSKOVIC	Rywka	1924	F	YV	
MOSKOVICZ	Samhuel	1908	M	YV	
MOSKOVICZ	Hannah	1884	F	YV	
MOSKOVICZ	Beila	1906	F	YV	
MOSKOVICZ	Itzhak		M	YV	
MOSKOVICZ	Chaim	1880	M	YV	
MOSKOVITZ	Esther	1877	F	YV	
MULLER	silvia	15/09/1929	F	YV	
MULLER	Gizella	6/01/1912	F	YV	
NEUFELD	Anna		F	YV	
NEUMAN	Ignac	24/06/1902	M	YV	
NEUMAN	Simon		M	YV	
PELEG	Lajos	20/03/1905	M	YV	
POPPER	Herman	28/9/1878	M	YV	
RADO	David		M	YV	
RADO	Redo		M	YV	

RAPAPORT	Hugo	1922	M	YV	
RAPAPORT	Alexander	1891	M	YV	
RAPAPORT	Etel	1890	F	YV	
REICH	Mozes	21/03/1905	M	YV	
REICH	Simcha	1890	M	YV	
REIMANOVA	Eugene	24/11/1928	M	YV	
RIEDER	David	1870	M	YV	
RODNER	Alice		F	YV	
ROSENBERG	Moric	6/01/1915	M	YV	
ROSENBERG	Lipa	1880	M	YV	
ROSENFELD	Adolf		M	YV	
ROSENFELD	Elisa		F	YV	
ROSNER	Jozef	1893	M	YV	
ROTH	Jozef	1929	M	YV	
ROTH	Bila	1936	F	YV	
ROTH	Bluma	1931	F	YV	
ROTH	Moric	1922	M	YV	
ROTH	Mendel	1898	M	YV	
ROTH	Moric	7/10/1886	M	YV	
ROTH	Yaakov	1933	M	YV	
ROTHMAN	Lemi		F	YV	
RUTHOVA	Edita	21/09/1923	F	YV	
SALAMON	Moor		M	YV	
SALAMON	Alexander		M	YV	
SALMON	Joshua	1921	M	YV	
SALOMON	Arza	1905	F	YV	
SALOMON	Shmuel	1881	M	YV	
SALOMON	Ida	1888	F	YV	
SALOMON	Ida	1924	F	YV	
SALOMON	Reiszel	1921	F	YV	
SCHONBERGER	Miksa	25/03/1905	M	YV	
SCHONEBERGER	Adolf	1932		YV	
SCHWAEBER	Laenka	10/4/1877	F	YV	
SCHWARZ	Sarah	1913	F	YV	
SHAEFFEROVA	Cervenka	1922	F	YV	
SHTAYNER	Peter		M	YV	
STENER	Rogi	1913	M	YV	
SRULOVIC	Herman	1888	M	YV	
SRULOVIC	Abraham		M	YV	
STEINER	Rogi	1913	M	YV	
STERN	Jeno	18/04/1922	M	YV	
SZUCKS	Margit	1876	F	YV	
SZULOWICZ	Jolana	1896	F	YV	
TANENBAUM	Margit	1905	F	YV	
TEITELBAUM	Jolan	1910	F	YV	
THOMAN	Fanny	31/12/1881	F	YV	
VAINBERGER	Imre	1943	M	YV	
VAINBERGER	Regina	1906	F	YV	
VAINBERGER	Aleks	1941	M	YV	
WEINBERGER	Blanka	1903	F	YV	
WEINBERGER	Joszef	9/03/1905	M	YV	

WEINBERGER	Joel	18/2/1883	M	YV	
WEINBERGER	Martin	3/07/1925	M	YV	
WEINMAN	Menachem				
WEINMAN	Sarah		F	YV	
WEINMAN	Bernath	14/09/1924	M	YV	
WEISS	Gittel		F	YV	
WEISS	Sarah		F	YV	
WEISS	Mordechai		M	YV	
WEISS	Abraham	1892	M	YV	
WEISS	Meir		M	YV	
WEISS	Abraham	1/08/1903	M	YV	
WEISS	Adolf	1899	M	YV	
WEISS	Hannah		F	YV	
WEISSBERGER	Helen	1912	F	YV	
WEISSMAN	Tobias	19/06/1911	M	YV	
WEISSMAN	Bernath	14/09/1924	M	YV	
WEISZ	Mose	1871	M	YV	
WIZNER	Yuno	1910		YV	
WIZNER	Charlotta	1884	F	YV	
WOLNER	Idit	1912	F	YV	

Bibliography

Avriel, Ehud. *Open the Gates*. New York: Atheneum, 1975.

Bauer, Yehuda. *The Brichah-She'erit Hapletah 1944-1948*. Jerusalem: Yad Vashem, 1990.

Bauer, Yehuda. *Out of the Ashes*. Oxford: Pergamon, 1989.

Bauer, Yehuda. *Flight and Rescue*. New York: Random House, 1970.

Bogner, Nachum Dr. *At the Mercy of Strangers*. Jerusalem: Yad Vashem, 2009.

Cohen, Jonathan. *The Great Escape of Polish Jews 1946-1947*, Jerusalem: Yad Vashem.

Dekel, Efraim. *Bri'ha: Flight to the Homeland*. New York: Herzl Press, 1972.

Deutchkron, Inga. *The Anonymous Donor from Caracas Reveals Himself*, Maariv Newspaper, April 23, 1982.

Dobroszycki Lucjan. "Survival of the Holocaust in Poland- A Portrait based on Jewish Committee Records 1944-1947." Published by M.E. Sharpe, Armonk, New York. USA.

Grobman, Alex. *Battling for Souls*. Jersey City, N.J: Ktav Publishing House, 2004.

Nachmani-Gafni, Emunah Dr. *Hidden Children in Poland,* Israel. Hebrew.

Herzog, Itzhak Levi. Testimony of Itzhak Levi, February16, 1950.

Joint Archives in Israel.

Kahana, Dawid Rabbi. *After the Deluge*. Jerusalem: 1981. Hebrew.

Kahana, Dawid Rabbi. *The Diary of the Ghetto of Lemberg*. Jerusalem: 1979.

Kochavi, Arieh J. *Post Holocaust Politics*. North Carolina Press. 2004.

Kokkonen, Susanna Dr. *Jewish Displaced Persons in Postwar Italy, 1945-1951*. 2008.

Kovner, Abba. *On The Narrow Bridge*. Tel Aviv: 1981. Hebrew.

Kurtz, Aaron David. *From Ashes to Live*. Israel 2002.

Livne, Anat. "The Joint participation in the activities of the Bricha and illegal Aliyah, 1945-1948 in Europe." Presented as an M.A degree dissertation thesis at Tel Aviv University. August 2004. Hebrew.

Lukes, Igor. *On the Edge of the Cold War*. Oxford Press, 2012.

Lukes, Igor. The Czech special services against American intelligence during the Cold War 1945-1948, Project Muse, Vol.1. Number 9. MIT Press. Winter 2007.

Marks, Jane. *The Hidden Children*. New York: Fawcet Columbine, 1993.

New York Post front page dated October 2 1945.

Pinkas Hakehilot -Yad Vashem.

Pfeffer,Maurice " Noch dem Bafraiung" and translated into French. Published by Kalman-Levy in 2008.

Rosner, Leo. *The Holocaust Remembered*. USA 1998, pp.97-100.

Szulc, Tad. *The Secret Alliance*. New York: Farrar, Straus and Giroux, 1991.

Shapiro. *Political Activities by Rabbi Herzog in Europe*. Jerusalem: Yad Vashem, Hebrew.

Shragai, Zalman. The Rescue Trip in Europe, report, Jerusalem 1947.

Slovas, Shulem Dr. The Katyn Forest, Maariv publishers, Yad Vashem.

Smok Martin - movie entitled "Brichah". Toman confirms in an interview that he received such a call from Masaryk.

Smok Martin – Documentary dealing with the Czech political trials.

Turkov, Jonas En Pologne. *Après la Liberation*. Written in Yiddish.

The recorded testimonies of Tziporah Inbar, Hawa Kleinman, Batia Eisenstein, David Danieli, Shlomo Korn and Orna Keret.

UNRRA archives in Israel.

Urad Documentace A vyestrovani Zlocinu Komunismu, Policie Ceskie Republky. Czech police documents pertaining to Communist regime crimes.

Warhaftig, Zorach. *The Uprooted Jewish Refugees and Displaced Persons after Liberation: From War to Peace*, Vol. 5 (New York: Institute of Jewish Affairs of the American Jewish Congress and World Jewish Congress, 1946.

Whitemore, Brian. The Globe and Mail (The Boston Globe) newspaper. Interview with one of the Czech adoptees searching for her past. Ms.Uzlova was interviewed in Prague on 23/6/2001.

Yad Vashem Archives.

Zertal, Idit. *From Catastrophe to Power: The Holocaust Survivors and the Emergence of Israel. California* University Press, 1998.

Interviews with Anna Neufeld, Awraham Rosenberg, Batia Eisenstein, David Danieli, Avishay Braverman, Leo Rosner, Shimshon Lang, William Leibner.

Index

The Partial List of Sobrance Jews in the Appendix starting on page 181 was not indexed in this list below. Also not indexed below are the list of children and escorts that were on the train that left Poland on August 21 1946.

A

Abrahamovics, 26
Abramovitz, 110
Amarant, 44, 53
Arazi, 47, 48, 49, 50, 51
Arens, 114
Auerbach, 53
Avigur, 47, 150
Avriel, 133, 135, 162, 163, 188
Ayalon, 153

B

Banar, 155
Barrocas, 164
Bauer, 39, 53, 70, 81, 128, 135, 163, 188
Becker, 77, 81
Bein, 60
Benes, 31, 32, 35, 36, 39, 40, 53, 126
Benjamin, 46, 185
Berger, 45, 53
Berman, 27, 34, 39, 55, 67
Blatberg, 153
Braunfeld, 12
Braverman, 32, 38, 172, 177, 180, 189
Breitbart, 153

C

Clementis, 29, 31
Cohen, 56, 61, 70, 82, 188

D

Danelski, 78
Danieli, 78, 79, 83, 95, 99, 189
Danielski, 78, 79, 95
Davidovitch, 138
de Paz, 51
Dekel, 188
Doron, 133, 153, 162
Drucker, 77, 81

E

Einhorn, 77, 95
Elefantova, 155
Eylenbur, 12

F

Findling, 56, 70
Freilinger, 32

G

Gafni, 128, 188
Gaynor, 2, 52, 56, 63, 65, 68, 113, 116, 118, 123, 125
Gaynor Israel Jacobson, 52, 63, 65
Gaynor Jacobson, 2, 56, 65, 113, 116, 118, 123, 125
Goberman, 121, 125
Gold, 93
Goldberg, 20, 158
Goldberger, 3, 12, 14, 18, 19, 20, 21, 22, 23, 24, 25, 27, 29, 30, 34, 39, 57, 129, 134, 147, 153, 158, 164, 165, 166, 173, 176, 177, 178, 180
Goldberger Toman, 179
Goldberger-Lebovic, 158
Goldberg-Rosenberg, 25
Goldman, 41
Gottwald, 5, 29, 31, 32, 65, 110, 113, 122, 126, 132, 133, 136, 138, 145, 146, 150, 154, 162
Govsman, 125
Greene, 70, 128
Grunfeld, 12, 13
Gutman, 14, 17, 25, 29, 30, 129, 148
Gutman/Toman, 1
Gutman-Toman, 154

H

Haft, 153
Haig, 6
Halevi Herzog, 71, 93
Heilbrun, 106
Hershkovic, 27, 67

Herzog, 71, 72, 76, 78, 80, 81, 82, 84, 85, 86, 93, 97, 102, 111, 112, 183, 188
Hocha, 27
Hooter, 46, 49

J

Jacobson, 2, 52, 63, 65, 66, 67, 68, 70, 82, 96, 97, 110, 113, 116, 120, 121, 122, 123, 124, 125, 126, 128, 132, 133, 134, 149, 150, 151, 155, 162, 168
Joseffovics, 26

K

Kadlac, 155
Kahana, 188
Kahane, 61, 77
Kalmanowicz, 75
Kass, 128
Kelerman, 53
Keller, 170
Kochavi, 53, 114, 188
Korn, 83, 189
Kovner, 44, 53, 188

L

Landau, 113
Lang, 48, 49, 51, 53, 189
Lantos, 168
Lavon, 123
Lebovic, 158
Lebovitc, 146
Leibner, 1, 38, 42, 53, 70, 99, 116, 189
Leibovitz, 20, 134
Levine, 134, 151, 152, 154
Lidowsky, 44, 53
Lubianer, 123
Lukes, 38, 147, 154, 188

M

Marinadi, 15, 18
Masaryk, 2, 5, 6, 31, 36, 63, 70, 110, 119, 126, 132, 133, 136, 146, 162, 189
Monardi, 164

N

Nejedly, 65
Neufeld, 27, 30, 34, 38, 39, 170, 189
Nosek, 5, 29, 31, 32, 33, 40, 65, 129, 132, 133, 137, 144, 146, 150, 155, 156, 162, 177

O

Oren, 161
Orenstein, 161
Osterman, 22, 23, 164

P

Podor, 153
Price, 1, 38, 39, 53, 180
Puchler, 137, 138, 139, 140, 141, 143, 144, 145, 146, 156

R

Rajk, 149, 161
Reicin, 32, 133, 135, 161, 162, 163
Reinzinger, 32, 135, 161, 163
Reissman, 153
Resnick, 166
Resnik, 51, 52, 176
Rifkind, 108, 109, 110
Rohan, 175, 176, 177
Rosenberg, 22, 23, 24, 40, 129, 138, 144, 145, 146, 147, 151, 155, 156, 159, 164, 189
Rosenberg-Goldberg, 147, 159
Rosensaft, 107
Rosner, 49, 53, 188, 189

S

Schiff, 41
Schwartz, 41, 42, 43, 52, 60, 63, 102, 123, 124, 134
Shragai, 99, 188
Siwek, 75
Slansky, 29, 31, 32, 136, 138, 139, 140, 141, 144, 145, 146, 150, 154, 161, 163
Smok, 2, 70, 128, 189
Sneh, 133, 162
Sobol, 80, 81
Sokol, 75
Spiner, 77, 95
Steinhardt, 110, 111
Sternbuch, 75, 77, 82, 93, 95
Surkiss, 46
Svoboda, 133, 135, 144, 162, 163
Swoboda, 32
Szulc, 2, 5, 32, 38, 39, 53, 57, 63, 66, 70, 99, 114, 117, 126, 128, 135, 136, 152, 154, 163, 188

T

Thoman, 12, 24, 25, 129, 134, 157, 158
Thoman-Goldberger, 129

Thomann, 20, 30, 31

Tiszo, 27

Toman, 1, 2, 3, 5, 6, 14, 17, 18, 20, 22, 23, 25, 26, 29, 30, 31, 32, 33, 34, 38, 40, 41, 56, 57, 63, 65, 67, 68, 70, 82, 84, 97, 106, 110, 113, 115, 117, 121, 122, 123, 124, 125, 126, 128, 129, 130, 132, 133, 134, 135, 136, 137, 138, 139, 141, 142, 143, 144, 145, 146, 147, 148, 149, 150, 151, 152, 153, 154, 155, 156, 158, 159, 161, 162, 164, 165, 166, 167, 168, 170, 171, 172, 173, 174, 175, 176, 177, 178, 189

Toman Gutman, 171, 172

Toman/Goldberger, 3, 17, 135, 159, 176

Toman-Goldberger, 1

Tzimend, 53

Tzuckerman, 44, 53, 57, 58, 59, 60, 81

W

Wasserman, 75

Weisblum, 95

Weissblum, 77

Wohlgelernter, 71, 75, 76, 93

Z

Zertal, 53, 189

Zindel, 106